Teaching the
Humanities Online

History, Humanities, and New Technology

Series Editors

David J. Staley
Director, Harvey Goldberg Center for Excellence in Teaching, Ohio State University

Jeffrey Barlow
Director, Berglund Center for Internet Studies, Pacific University

Dennis A. Trinkle
Provost and Chief Academic Officer, Harrison College

**COMPUTERS, VISUALIZATION, AND HISTORY:
HOW NEW TECHNOLOGY WILL TRANSFORM OUR
UNDERSTANDING OF THE PAST**
David J. Staley

**DIGITAL SCHOLARSHIP IN THE TENURE, PROMOTION,
AND REVIEW PROCESS**
Edited by Deborah Lines Andersen

TEACHING HISTORY IN THE DIGITAL CLASSROOM
D. Antonio Cantu and Wilson J. Warren

VIDEOGAMES AND EDUCATION
Harry J. Brown

Teaching the Humanities Online

A Practical Guide
to the Virtual Classroom

Steven J. Hoffman, editor

M.E.Sharpe
Armonk, New York
London, England

Library of Congress Cataloging-in-Publication Data

Teaching the humanities online : a practical guide to the virtual classroom / edited by Steven
J. Hoffman.
 p. cm.— (History, humanities, and new technology)
 Includes bibliographical references and index.
 ISBN 978-0-7656-2081-1 (cloth : alk. paper)—ISBN 978-0-7656-2082-8 (pbk. : alk. paper)
 1. Humanities—Study and teaching. 2. Humanities—Study and teaching—Technological
innovations. 3. Web-based instruction. 4. Distance education. I. Hoffman, Steven J.

AZ182.T43 2010
001.3′071—dc22   2010021694

Printed in the United States of America

The paper used in this publication meets the minimum requirements of
American National Standard for Information Sciences
Permanence of Paper for Printed Library Materials,
ANSI Z 39.48-1984.

♾

| IBT (c) | 10 | 9 | 8 | 7 | 6 | 5 | 4 | 3 | 2 | 1 |
| IBT (p) | 10 | 9 | 8 | 7 | 6 | 5 | 4 | 3 | 2 | 1 |

Contents

Acknowledgments

This book grew out of the relationships and discussions fostered by the American Association for History and Computing. The then executive director, David J. Staley, approached me about editing a book dealing with online teaching in the humanities. Kelly Robison was instrumental in focusing the initial conception of the project and assisted in drafting the call for proposals. The friendship and support of colleagues on the editorial board of the *Journal of the Association for History and Computing*, particularly Deborah Lines Andersen, Jessica Lacher-Feldman, and Bud Burkhard, and the editors of the series *History, Humanities, and New Technology*, David J. Staley, Jeffrey Barlow, and Dennis A. Trinkle, have been instrumental in keeping me sane throughout my own adventures in the world of teaching with technology and, in particular, in the development and completion of this manuscript. Special thanks to Valerie Rake, who provided insightful feedback on an earlier version of this manuscript.

I would be remiss not to thank the people at my own institution, Southeast Missouri State University, who have supported my efforts to explore the ways in which technology and history can be integrated meaningfully into the work we all do as both teachers and learners. In particular, I would like to thank David Starrett, who frequently found funding to support my various efforts and who was not above using friendship to get me to do things with technology and teaching I might not have done otherwise. I also need to thank Daryl Fridley, whose good-natured friendship has sustained me in more ways than he knows, and whose work appears in this volume.

As with any effort of this kind, the people who have contributed in one way or another to the successful completion of this book are really too numerous to mention. Special thanks, though, must go to the contributors of this volume, whose patience, good humor, and perseverance throughout the publication process have been greatly appreciated. I am also indebted to my editors at M.E. Sharpe, Steven Drummond and Patricia Kolb, without whose support and guidance this book would never have seen the light of day, and to Laurie Lieb and Henrietta Toth who helped make the manuscript immeasurably better than it would have been without them.

For unfailing encouragement, support, and seemingly complete acceptance of the many things I do, including the countless hours poured into producing this manuscript, I thank my family, Margaret Waterman and Russell Hoffman.

Lastly, I have been privileged and honored to work with a truly remarkable colleague, the person who introduced me to the world of technology and teaching and whose support, insight, and guidance have helped me become a better person and a better teacher, both online and off. This book is dedicated to Larry Easley, mentor and friend.

Introduction

The Future Is Now

Steven J. Hoffman

By any measure, online education in the United States has entered the mainstream. Online education will continue to see rapid growth in the near term, and delivery of online courses will become an increasingly important part of the long-term strategies of all institutions of higher learning. Until very recently, teaching a course over the Internet was called "distance education." We can no longer think of online education as distance education, which implies that the only market for such classes is students physically distant from colleges and universities. While there are still many students for whom a university is physically inaccessible, an increasing number of students taking online courses do so for reasons of "temporal accessibility." Especially for many working adults, single parents, and overseas military personnel, online courses allow them the flexibility to fit higher education into their schedules and circumstances. Indeed, many students today taking online courses already attend a bricks-and-mortar school.

Online education will not displace traditional face-to-face instruction, but will surely occupy an important niche in the expanding market for higher education. This means that more and more courses will migrate from traditional face-to-face lecture halls and classrooms into digital learning environments. This migration will necessarily affect teaching and learning in the humanities disciplines, resulting in courses that either are fully online or exist in some sort of blended environment with both face-to-face and online components. Providing faculty members with the tools and information they need to navigate this transition successfully is the subject of this book.

Teaching and learning in an online environment is not the same experience as a face-to-face class; professors cannot simply transfer their lecture notes into an online environment and expect the same learning outcomes. Online teaching and learning are built from different pedagogical assumptions and require different pedagogical strategies. Faculty members who are contemplating or beginning to teach online are the main audience for this work. Teaching the humanities, either online or face-to-face, is far different from teaching the natural sciences, and this volume will attempt to address teaching online from this perspective.

The present volume will discuss the differences between online and face-to-face learning environments and will assess and evaluate best practices in developing and teaching online courses. Drawing on the expertise of teachers of the humanities who have deep experiences in the online environment, this work explores a variety of areas within the online teaching experience. Because the humanities constitute such a broad arena, we have consciously tried to incorporate multiple perspectives into this work, addressing similar topics from the viewpoint of different disciplines. When Congress established the National Endowment for the Humanities in 1965, it defined the humanities as a set of academic disciplines including

> language, both modern and classical; linguistics; literature; history; jurisprudence; philosophy; archaeology; comparative religion; ethics; the history, criticism and theory of the arts; those aspects of social sciences which have humanistic content and employ humanistic methods; and the study and application of the humanities to the human environment with particular attention to reflecting our diverse heritage, traditions, and history and to the relevance of the humanities to the current conditions of national life.[1]

In the spirit of this multidisciplinary perspective on the human experience, we have invited essays from authors in different disciplines for the topics covered in this volume. As a result, we have contributions from faculty members teaching in art education, communication, English, history, social studies education, and interdisciplinary studies departments, as well as directors of writing centers and online education and distance learning programs.

We are well aware that because advances in technology continue at a rapid pace and new developments and products to enhance online teaching become available seemingly all the time, we run the risk of offering what may seem like outdated advice. In a world where one can find the latest information available for instant consumption on the Internet, the idea of producing a print manuscript to inform about online matters may seem quaint. An undeniable problem we face is that the long process involved in bringing a volume like this to press sometimes works against our ability to include the most up-to-date information regarding available technology. But since this volume is not really about the technology, but instead focuses on thinking about the ways in which available technologies can be used to enhance our teaching in both synchronous and asynchronous forums, we believe it will still be worth the read many years from now—even in the face of rapid technological change.

To begin, we find that too often colleges and universities, faculty members, and students fail to ask the initial question of whether or not they are ready to engage in online teaching and learning. Addressing this issue in Chapter 1, Khadijah O. Miller examines the questions instructors and students should ask themselves when preparing to move into the realm of online teaching and learning.

For those who have made the decision to go online, Chapter 2 explores the methods for effective course design. Faculty members cannot simply make their notes available online. They must structure a learning experience for students in ways that are different from the traditional face-to-face classroom experience. With an eye toward reducing the distance in online classes, Lisa M. Lane shares the latest research in presentation and social interaction styles and explores other techniques to help instructors make their courses more active, interesting, and effective.

Since course management systems often play such an important role in structuring how a class is presented online, we offer two essays exploring this topic. In Chapter 3 Sharmila Pixy Ferris and Maureen C. Minielli examine course management systems from a pedagogical perspective. The authors look at the basics of electronic courseware, explain relevant terminology, and describe the various functions found in the most popular types of electronic courseware, all with the goal of assisting faculty with varying degrees of technical expertise to use these important systems to promote effective teaching and learning. Chapter 4 follows the same theme, but provides practical advice for moving beyond the basics and not letting "the tools in one's toolbox determine what one builds." In this chapter, Lisa M. Lane shows how course management systems can be effectively managed to promote pedagogical goals and achieve more effective teaching and learning.

Chapter 5 explores the characteristics and benefits of the blended classroom to highlight the advantages gained by incorporating online components in a classroom course. Drawing on the notion of social capital and the importance of face-to-face interaction, Peter Sands argues persuasively that blended courses offer the best of both worlds—the flexibility of online learning and the value-added benefit of gathering together in the same place at the same time to debate and discuss the issues of the day.

Facilitating interaction between faculty and students in the online environment is the topic of the next three chapters. In Chapter 6, Michelle Kilburn shows how instructors can establish a successful collaborative learning environment online by addressing student-to-content, student-to-instructor, student-to-student, and student-to-interface connections. Chapter 7 explores how using the tools of social media can enhance interaction by taking teachers into the world of their students. Allen C. Gathman and Mary Harriet Talbut explain the basics of using Facebook as a means of developing community with students in online, blended, or face-to-face courses and explore the ways in which other kinds of social networking tools such as Ning, wikis, blogs, Twitter, and Chat, among others, can help instructors achieve their teaching and learning goals online.

As all instructors know, engaging students in meaningful online discussion is more involved than simply requiring a minimum number of posts. What happens when a student posts something inappropriate or perhaps presents material that is simply wrong? In Chapter 8, Melanie L. Buffington explores various ways in which faculty can engage students in meaningful online discussion; she also explains how dealing with issues regarding inappropriate or inaccurate comments is similar to and different from the interaction that occurs in face-to-face classes.

In Chapter 9, Daryl E. Fridley conducts a tour of the web, showing how instructors can use this virtual library to enhance their teaching and learning. This is a chapter you may wish to read with an Internet-connected computer close at hand so that you can discover for yourself that using this resource is not so different from what you are probably already doing when you seek information and material to use in your classes; it is, as Daryl suggests, "easier than it looks."

We turn, in Chapter 10, to the issues of assessing the online learner in a meaningful and authentic fashion. In the online environment every test is a take-home test and is likely to be an open-book test as well. In this chapter, Martha Henckell focuses attention on what constitutes learning, discusses how assessment can lead to more effective teaching, and explores a variety of assessment tools and techniques that will enable instructors to assess learning effectively in the online environment.

In Chapter 11, I address faculty concerns about making the move to teaching online and describe what institutions can do to promote faculty involvement in the creation and delivery of online courses. In Chapter 12, David J. Staley imagines the future directions of online education in the humanities, suggesting five trends that will influence the world of online teaching and learning well into the twenty-first century.

Online teaching and learning in the humanities is here to stay. We hope the essays in this volume will assist instructors who want to learn more about making the transition to online teaching. Although this collection of essays is specifically aimed at faculty members and administrators new to the online experience, we also hope it will be a useful tool for more experienced users as well. The collected insights, suggestions, and prior experiences of the online faculty collected here represent the best advice from colleagues who have scouted out the territory ahead. We wish you luck as you embark on your own journey into the future, and we encourage you to pick your way through the chapters in this book and join us in the exciting world of teaching and learning online . . . because the future is now, and it is time to get started.

Note

1. "Who We Are," National Endowment for the Humanities, www.neh.gov/whoweare/overview.html.

Teaching the Humanities Online

Before We Begin

Preparing to Teach Online

Khadijah O. Miller

Online education in the humanities calls for a great deal of preparation before the instructor and students enter the course site. This preparation involves acquisition of basic technical prowess, assessment of student learning styles, pedagogical style selection, content review and adaptation, and implementation. To prepare effectively, it is necessary to consider: Who is the online instructor? Who is the online student? What tools are needed? What time is required? What facilities and resources are available? What skills are needed? What learning styles are addressed (or left out)? Who is served best by online education?

Technical Prowess

To teach online effectively, the instructor cannot simply transfer face-to-face lecture notes into a PowerPoint presentation or a Word document to be downloaded and read. The online instructor first needs to be comfortable with technology—the computer, various software, the course management system, video and audio. The online instructor is not required to be a technology expert. Content is most important, but effective online delivery of the content is the responsibility of the instructor.

What is required of the instructor is some basic knowledge of electronic media and comfort in using various formats. The combined access to media (the Internet, processes, programs, etc.) and technical knowledge (hardware, software programs, formats, etc.) reinforces the shift in the instructor's role in the learning environment from teacher-directed learning to student-centered learning. The online classroom becomes an online knowledge center where the student and teacher capture, share, store, access, and create knowledge. The online instructor thus serves as a facilitator, assisting in the development and presentation of knowledge media and course content knowledge.

This new role as facilitator may require the instructor to work with technical experts to maximize the effective exchange of knowledge in this delivery mode. Ideally, the online instructor should work with an instructional designer and a course management specialist to create and operate the course management site. This allows the instructor to focus on content and to share implementation ideas. However, in most cases the instructor wears multiple hats—dealing with content, delivery, operation, and maintenance of the course site.

In wearing these multiple hats, the online instructor works to balance the focus on course content with the concern for effective content delivery. In a traditional classroom the instructor lectures, writes notes on the board, pauses for questions, answers questions, engages in dialogues, and involves students in various interactive methods of teaching, learning, and exchanging knowledge. The online environment can offer an instructor these same opportunities, but in a different way and through multiple media. What is most needed, once the instructor decides to commit to teaching online, is technical support. This technical support assists in maximizing the learning experience in the course for the students and the instructor.

The first challenge many instructors face is the unknown: What will happen to my lectures? Where will my work go? Will I still have control, even in cyberspace? What about my intellectual property rights? These valid questions, in addition to the technical challenges posed by online teaching, often cause resistance in faculty considering going online.

Once these concerns are addressed and resolved, another challenge that will surface is the idea that this format could eliminate our worth as instructors: "If everything we teach is on the computer, what are we needed for?" Instructors are needed, as they are pertinent to the facilitation of course content and knowledge. Even in an era of budget restraints and cuts, instructors (aka facilitators) are needed to ensure that learning and engagement occurs. The time, effort, patience, commitment, and study that online media education (aka eLearning) requires of instructors often does not receive the recognition it deserves in academia. Support, promotion, tenure recognition, and appropriate consideration and credit to online instructors and their instruction need to increase in order to decrease the reluctance of instructors to begin this process of teaching online.

Once the instructor is ready to embark upon online teaching, the following questions should be asked:

- Why do I want to teach online? Is it through online education, perhaps, that teaching and learning can be improved? Will it enhance my own knowledge as well as increase student engagement and practice of course content?
- My department is developing an online program and I am obligated to participate. What are the goals of the program? Do I subscribe to them? How many of my colleagues are involved as well? How will the courses I teach fit with the other online courses? Can my course be taught effectively online? Is collaboration with other faculty members possible?
- Am I committed? Do I have or will I make the time to learn, develop, and use the technology and teaching methods required? Are there any resources to assist in this shift?
- What vision do I have for the online course? What aspects of my face-to-face teaching can easily transfer to an online environment? Will this course replace my face-to-face offering? Or will it merely provide a different method for taking the class? Is it possible to offer a hybrid course? Is this course required? What can I do in this learning mode to enhance learning and increase engagement? Transitioning from face-to-face to online teaching requires instructors to revisit and often revise the ways that teaching is approached and delivered.
- What resources are available to assist in this process? Is there technical support available—an instructional designer, a course management system specialist? Does my institution have an office or department of eLearning or technology? If so, what services does it provide?
- Will I get release time? What will be the faculty/student ratio online? What technology is available to me as an instructor and what technology is accessible to students? Are there any incentives for teaching online?
- What do I need to learn? What (new) technology skills are needed? What (new) teaching methods are needed? How can I learn them? Do I have the time to learn these new technology skills and develop new instructional methods?
- What is my plan? What is my timeline for creating the course? How can it be executed effectively and efficiently?

- Will I be recognized and/or rewarded for the time and energies invested to create an online course?

Student Learning Style

The instructor needs to be mindful of the online student. Most online students juggle multiple responsibilities. They usually do not have the physical time to sit in a classroom at a particular time for a specific length of time. They need the flexibility of reading and writing at two o'clock in the morning, or whenever they have allotted or designated time to study. They also need to self-evaluate and assess whether the online learning environment is right for them. Several online student preassessments ask basic questions of the online student regarding technological knowledge and access as well as maturity level and time availability. Many institutions offer these assessments through their eLearning programs.

Although students may have no other practical option, if they are to continue their education online, they still need to ask and answer certain questions:

- What is my learning style? Am I an auditory, visual, or kinesthetic learner?
- Do I want to learn online? Why? Why not?
- Do I own a computer? Do I have access to the necessary equipment (hardware and software) to be successful online?
- Do I have a physical learning space that I can devote to online education?
- How much time can I devote to this online learning experience? Can I manage my time well? What is my online weekly learning schedule?
- Do I have access to and know how to contact technical assistance?
- Am I self-motivated? Am I an aggressive learner? Will I seek assistance and ask questions of my instructor and classmates? Can I initiate conversations and dialogue to maximize this online learning experience?

As instructors approach the online educational environment, it is important for them to be cognizant of what has led students to this mode of learning. Tasks and schedules should be designed to effectively maximize students' participation and time put into the course.

Pedagogical Style Selection

Pedagogy and the teaching methods for the content are most important. The online pedagogy, the art and study of teaching methods, focusing on the goals of teaching (how they should and can be met) and how the recipient meets or is assisted in meeting those educational goals and objectives, has to be a part of the getting-started phase. There are numerous theories about the ways in which learning takes place, including adult learning theories, constructivist and objectivist paradigms, Bloom's taxonomy (1956), problem-based learning (Bridges and Hallinger 1992), and the engagement theory (Kearsley and Shneiderman 1998). Chickering and Garnson's "Seven Principles for Good Practice in Undergraduate Education" (1987) serves as a practical checklist for instructional environments, particularly online.

In *The Adult Learner: A Neglected Species* (1984), Malcolm Knowles shifted the meaning of "andragogy" to derive a broader definition of a learner-focused education for people of all ages. This model meets multiple needs, including letting learners know why something is important, assisting them to direct themselves through information, and relating the topic to the learner's experiences. It also recognizes that most people will not learn until they are ready and self-motivated to learn. For instance, when considering this pedagogy with the course content and learning objectives, a thematic history course (e.g., a course about the civil rights movement) would be a good example. Students can make clear-cut connections to the activities, motives, circumstances, people, and places during the civil rights movement that have distinct effects on the life they live today. They can also make a clear statement why these connections are important and relate the history to their own lives and learning experiences.

The objectivist and constructivist approaches or paradigms are seen as two extremes. However, in the context of online learning, all paradigms must be considered for the diverse, broad, and multiple learners in this educational setting. According to objectivists, the learner strives for complete and correct understanding of the multiple structures (entities, properties, etc.) in the world. The constructivist paradigm argues that knowledge is contextual with multiple meanings and perspectives for any and every experience, concept, or event; hence, meaning is derived from that particular experience. Bloom's taxonomy provides a pedagogical framework that categorizes various levels of content attainment abstraction (listed from lowest to highest level): knowledge, comprehension, application, analysis, synthesis, and evaluation.

When considering the objectivist or constructivist approach, instructors should consider the level of the course. Objectivist pedagogy usually works best in a lower-level survey course, where students need to attain, retain, and recall facts, events, dates, people, and places, focusing on chronology. Here, objective online exams and quizzes (i.e., with multiple-choice, true-or-false, and fill-in questions) can be constructed to affirm students' progress and grasp of complete and correct information, structures, and timelines. This pedagogy works well in core general education courses, including history, sociology, political science, psychology, philosophy, and Western or Eastern civilizations.

The constructivist approach is most effective in upper-level courses that call for students to deal with experiential and application-based assumptions and perspectives. The constructivist approach may work best in a theory-based literature course online where students need to evaluate and relate context (historical, social, and political) to the readings and their own lives. This approach, which pulls from the higher levels of Bloom's taxonomy, works well in interdisciplinary studies, English literature, and critical-thinking-based courses.

Problem-based learning (PBL) starts learning with problems for students to solve, discuss, and dissect. It is considered a professional preparation strategy that is multifaceted and cross-disciplinary. With PBL, students learn concepts, theories, strategies, terms, and paradigms to assist them in finding solutions. The problems are usually similar to the ones students will face in their particular professions. This approach works well in courses that require students to call on prior content knowledge and is best delivered in scenarios often found in discussion-based online learning (i.e., discussion boards, virtual classrooms, and chats—all of which are discussed later in this book). In an online environment, the PBL approach works well in courses that focus on application, analysis, synthesis, and evaluation (the higher-order thinking aspects of Bloom's taxonomy).

The engagement theory calls for learners to be actively engaged in meaningful tasks in order for effective learning to occur. Engagement theory calls for all learning to have three major characteristics: collaboration, a problem-based approach, and authenticity. This theory utilizes elements from the other pedagogical theories, recognizing that multiple approaches to teaching are conducive to optimal effective learning.

Chickering and Gamson's (1987) seven principles are all based on good practice:

1. Good practice encourages contact between students and faculty.
2. Good practice develops reciprocity and cooperation among students.
3. Good practice uses active learning techniques.
4. Good practice gives students prompt feedback.
5. Good practice emphasizes time on task.
6. Good practice communicates high expectations.
7. Good practice respects diverse talents and ways of learning.

Another useful guide for developing an informed and effective online learning environment is Robert Gagne's "Nine Events of Instruction" described in *The Conditions of Learning and Theory of Instruction* (1985). These nine steps or events with corresponding cognitive processes can be easily applied in developing a course site:

1. Gain attention (reception)
2. Inform students of the objectives (expectancy)
3. Use recall (retrieval)
4. Present the material (selective perception)
5. Provide learning guidance (semantic encoding)
6. Elicit performance (responding)
7. Provide feedback (reinforcement)
8. Assess performance (retrieval)
9. Enhance retention and transfer (generalization)

All these pedagogical approaches assist students to reach a particular educational goal. The common thread in each is student-centeredness. Online education requires a student-focused learning environment. The online instructor's choice of pedagogical approach should be appropriate to the learners. Is this a class with working parents as students? Is this a lower-level survey or a higher-level course? Is it self-paced? Is this a course for freshmen students who are still getting acclimated to college? Or is it a course for second- and third-year students who have already been exposed to some online learning?

Content Review and Adaptation

The humanities are the branches of knowledge that concern themselves with human beings—their history, culture, language, literature, arts, and philosophy. The methodology often includes an analytical and critical method of inquiry. Unlike in the natural biological and physical sciences, questions and answers in the humanities are not always clear-cut. Often there is no one solution to a question, and multiple formulas may be needed to holistically cover all that is involved.

The humanities serve as a wonderful, fertile ground for developing online education because of the multiple venues to present content. For example, in a fine arts course, virtual tours of museums and other cultural venues assist students learning about artistic form and presentation. The use of a drawing program can also enhance the learning experience. Other possibilities to consider in presenting content include alternatives to written text. For example, in addition to reading Martin Luther King Jr.'s "Letter from Birmingham Jail," students can listen to an audio clip of the speech and then watch documentary footage of events in Birmingham during the same time period. Here, instructors use technology to enhance their students' understanding of history. Other modes to consider include audio lectures, videos, animation, simulations, music and sound clips, visual graphic presentations, and virtual tours. National Public Radio, Public Broadcasting System, C-Span, and other nonprofit organizations offer a plethora of online educational resources for the humanities to enhance learning and engage students online.

Instructors should review their traditional face-to-face content delivery methods and seek to re-create those that are most interactive, engaging, thought provoking, and substantial. For those modes that are less engaging, the online educational environment provides an opportunity to create new ways to facilitate and encourage student learning. This environment also allows students to take greater responsibility for their learning. Instructors should ask their students what modes of delivery for content they prefer. Once a course is up and running, there will be changes, refinements, eliminations, and additions that improve the online course.

Implementation

Many institutions have student orientation checklists and online course readiness assessments for students to complete before registering for an online course. Unfortunately, they often do not offer such a checklist for instructors.

Implementing online teaching within the humanities takes patience, skill, and common sense. Instructors (and students) should be prepared for a learning experience. Many instructors teaching online, including the author of this chapter, jumped in without asking questions or getting answers to many of the questions in this chapter until they were forced to do so. The criteria necessary to effectively implement an online course may shift from discipline to discipline as well as from institution to institution. Class size, course load, and content must be considered. How can an instructor effectively teach forty first-year students in a 100-level history survey course online? How much interaction and engagement is expected and needed? A key element in any online course, at any level, is clarity of the instructor's intentions and directions. Instructors may have the best intentions at heart, but if those intentions are not carefully specified and made easily accessible by the students, what good are they?

Instructors should be assessing the effectiveness of their instruction both during and after the course. By comparing their teaching in the physical classroom and in the virtual classroom—and its effectiveness—they can make adjustments. Instructors should expect to teach their course online multiple times. It often takes several terms of teaching to figure out how to implement their pedagogy effectively, cover the necessary content completely, and engage their students in this production-based learning environment.

As instructors approach their computers and turn the switch on, it is imperative that they ask, "Should I even begin?" If the answer is yes, then they should dive in headfirst with eyes open. They need to remember that teaching online is an ongoing learning activity. Online instructors should let their content knowledge, technical prowess, and appropriate pedagogy drive decisions, while being mindful of institutional and departmental demands, criteria, and requirements.

The online environment provides fertile ground for presenting to students human life events, activities, and thoughts in a myriad of venues—art, words, song, dance, lecture, reenactments, film, radio, and television. In the online environment, students can be connected to events across the globe, which they may not have been privy to before. This environment also presents a new mode of teaching and learning as the instructor takes on a facilitator role.

The online world is shifting the ways we teach and learn. Through technology, we can present data in new and dynamic ways, helping students to develop a deeper understanding of a topic in a well-structured online environment. The quality of that experience depends on the instructor who accepts the challenge of facilitating student-directed, production-based learning.

References

Bloom, Benjamin S. 1956. *A Taxonomy of Educational Objectives, Handbook 1: Cognitive Domain*. 2nd ed. Reading, PA: Addison Wesley.

Bridges, Edwin M., and Philip Hallinger. 1992. *Problem-Based Learning for Administrators*. Eugene, OR: ERIC Clearinghouse on Educational Management.

Chickering, Arthur W., and Zelda Gamson. 1987. "Seven Principles of Good Practice in Undergraduate Education." Originally published in *AAHE Bulletin*. http://honolulu.hawaii.edu/intranet/committees/FacDevCom/guidebk/teachtip/7princip.htm.

Draves, William A. 2002. *Teaching Online*. 2nd ed. River Falls, WI: LERN Books.

Gagne, Robert. 1985. *The Conditions of Learning and Theory of Instruction*. 4th ed. New York: Holt, Rinehart and Winston.

Kearsley, Greg, and Ben Shneiderman. 1998. "Engagement Theory: A Framework for Technology-Based Teaching and Learning." *Educational Technology* 38, no. 5. http://home.sprynet.com/~gkearsley/engage.htm.

Knowles, Malcolm. 1984. *The Adult Learner: A Neglected Species*. 3rd ed. Houston, TX: Gulf.

Waterhouse, Shirley. 2005. *The Power of eLearning: The Essential Guide for Teaching in the Digital Age*. Boston: Pearson.

Additional Reading

Bollinger, Doris U., and Oksana Wasilik. 2009. "Factors Influencing Faculty Satisfaction with Online Teaching and Learning in Higher Education." *Distance Education* 30, no. 1: 103–116.

Deal, Walter F. 2002. "Distance Learning: Teaching Technology Online." *Technology Teacher* (May/June): 21–26.

Paulus, Trena M., Brian Horvitz, and Min Shi. 2006. "Isn't It Just Like Our Situation? Engagement and Learning in an Online Story-Based Environment." *Educational Technology Research and Development* 54, no. 4: 355–385.

Rasmussen, Karen L., Joyce Coleman Nichols, and Fernaundra Ferguson. 2006. "It's a New World: Multiculturalism in a Virtual Environment." *Distance Education* 27, no. 2: 265–278.

Shin, Namin, and Jason K.Y. Chan. 2004. "Direct and Indirect Effects of Online Learning on Distance Education." *British Journal of Educational Technology* 35, no. 3: 275–288.

Young, Jeffrey R. 2009. "In Case of Emergency, Break Tradition: Teach Online." *Chronicle of Higher Education*, September 4, A23–A24.

Reducing Distance in Online Classes

Lisa M. Lane

Distance education has a long history, but most humanities instructors come to it from the classroom rather than correspondence courses or telecourses. Online teaching is clearly different from classroom teaching, and for many novice instructors the difference seems extreme. Everything seems somehow removed from the usual teaching experience. Instead of direct and personal contact, there is email and messaging. Instead of presenting a lecture and sensing the mood of the room, there are webpages of text to be "posted" (as if they were being mailed to the other side of the globe). The Internet, or a template in a course management system, is the new "classroom." The process of course redesign thus takes place in a far different space than classroom teaching, and it is easy to get tangled in the technology, to start by figuring out how to pack in assignments, readings, and tests. There is a tendency to ignore the uncomfortable reality: that online teachers and students are separated by distance, a distance of both space and time. Teachers and students experience feelings of isolation and disconnect that can affect motivation and skills acquisition (Joyce and Brawon 2009). All participants benefit from efforts to "prevent the emotional and cognitive disconnection" that students experience in an online environment (Lewis and Abdul-Hamid 2006, 96). Reducing this distance must be a priority in order to create a successful online class.

The Instructor as Social Presence: Reducing Student-Instructor Distance

The most important factor in reducing distance is instructor presence. If students feel the instructor is really there, self-motivation is supported and retention increased. Instructor presence can be created in several ways, but requires that the instructor be comfortable with both the chosen pedagogy and the web environment itself.

Pedagogical approach must be chosen carefully. The initial challenge for classroom instructors is translating their teaching method into an online environment. Those who are most comfortable with lecturing at the front of the room often begin by typing out or audio recording their lectures or creating slideshows with narration. Discussion facilitators tend to look at a discussion forum or social networking site as a starting point. Constructivists often begin with a blog or wiki, seeking a space where students can create things. It is the pedagogical approach that should determine these choices.

Although the technology can seem overwhelming, instructors must understand that the technology never really determines the teaching—it is the instructor's *approach* to the technology that matters. Any course management system, or any open website, can be adapted for educational use. Starting with a pedagogical goal, a definite preferred approach or direction to the subject and material, allows the instructor to focus on creating an effective class. Over the past decade, many techniques have emerged for designing classes, yet most instructors are simply given a template or perhaps a blank class in a course management system. After looking at such an example, they may feel that there is not much to learn about course design: they just need to follow the model, plugging in the specific content. However, to think "All I have to do is learn Blackboard" or "I'll purchase this course cartridge that goes with my textbook and all will be well" is to severely limit one's options, and it invariably creates a disconnect between instructor and student. The "plug and play" approach increases distance because it is as if the instructor were offering a class without the classroom experience. The best way to avoid it is to focus on the pedagogy, while adapting to the environment of the Internet.

Professional development thus takes on a different direction for online instructors. In addition to attending conferences and reading articles in their discipline, they must "attend" and "read" the web to become accustomed to their new classroom. This "serious play," the time spent exploring the web, trying out programs and websites, is done with teaching in mind. For example, collecting articles and blog posts in their discipline can create a convenient list of resources, while also providing the experience of social bookmarking, which students could do as part of the class. Creating a slideshow or podcast for a class can encourage self-sufficiency in the instructor and also generate interest in having students create such presentations. Most non-educators go online for the first time to access information and communicate, reducing the distance among friends and family. Engaging in such activities can give professors a feel for the web as a social space, a space for interaction.

The most important benefit of online social networking is the conscious creation of an online persona. In determining what information to share with friends and which slideshows or videos to post in public, web users naturally set boundaries for themselves and determine where on the web they feel comfortable, and in what guise. Some online instructors reveal a great deal about themselves in an online environment, while others are more circumspect. This is similar to teacher behavior in a physical classroom, and it lets students know how accessible the instructor is and what kinds of interactions are appropriate. Instructors who chat about their kids on a social networking site, but are more formal and discipline-oriented in the "classroom" space send a message to students about both their availability and what constitutes appropriate online interaction for learning. The persona an instructor creates can be highly professional, but still very "real." An instructor's personality must come through to reach students, to let them know that an actual person is at the other end of the wire. Otherwise the tendency is for the course to feel automated, and the student unnecessary to the process, which leads to high drop rates.

Understanding Web Learning: Reducing User-Environment Distance

Instructor presence is particularly important since connecting people has become a main purpose of the Internet. Awareness of this intimidates some instructors, however. Today's students seem to engage in social media regularly, sharing their lives and ambitions with others over the Internet, often in a more open way than may seem appropriate. The assumption is that since students, especially younger students, spend so much time online, they must know more than we do about this environment.

The perception of college students as tech-savvy "digital natives," a term coined by Marc Prensky (2001), was encouraged in a number of publications during the late 1990s and early 2000s. Among these was the EDUCAUSE book *Educating the Net Generation* (Oblinger and Oblinger 2005), which claimed that Net Gen'ers needed differ-ent stimuli than students in older generations in order to learn because they had certain generational tendencies related to technology. These habits included scanning text and being frustrated by long blocks of text, processing images quickly, multitasking (the "hypertext" mind), and handling multiple sensory inputs simultaneously. The challenge of teaching these media-saturated, multitasking students was to try to establish habits of mind that encouraged deep learning, while creating materials and activities acknowledging their different thinking processes. The point was made that today's students, unlike their instructors who generally come from older generations, are media-savvy and technically skilled twenty-first-century individuals, but they have instructors using antiquated, twentieth-century methods.

This perspective is increasingly being shown to be wrong. Current studies show that even younger students are not very adept even at ordinary desktop applications they have been taught to use (Grant, Malloy, and Murphy 2009). Not many of them blog or collect RSS (Really Simple Syndication) feeds or create web content, though 80 percent consider themselves highly skilled in using the Internet (Smith, Salaway, and Caruso 2009). Their expectations for learning with technology are low: they value the convenience of online classes but prefer face-to-face instruction (Pedró 2009, 17). The difference is that younger students use technology to interact socially far more frequently than students or teachers from older generations. But social use does not translate directly into educational use—it does not mean that these students are "capable of employing technology strategically to optimize learning experiences and outcomes" (Pedró 2009, 25). Even if they use the Internet to post photos or stay in touch with friends, this does not mean they know how to learn online. Nor does it mean they have the discipline to work in that environment. The instructor's role is not just to model expertise in an academic discipline, but also to model effective use of the online environment for learning.

The persistence of the "digital native" paradigm has also led to a reexamination of learning styles in a distance education context. In the past quarter century, there has been a lot of research about the way people learn. In 1983, Harvard professor Howard Gardner developed the idea that people have many different kinds of intelligences: spatial, musical, social, self, nature, language, logic/math, and kinesthetic. Working inside one's "preferred" style creates greater connection to what is being taught, while working in a less preferred style can increase the feeling of distance or isolation. While Gardner's book created a greater understanding of students' learning methods, there is little evidence that catering to such styles (by providing a movie to watch instead of reading text, for example) actually increases learning (Pashler et al. 2009). This is probably because although learning-style-based instruction can encourage students to strengthen already strong aptitudes, it does not stretch their ability to learn in different ways.

Nevertheless, understanding learning styles can be useful; it can change the way teachers view their own work and lead to a greater variety of approaches. A class that encourages students to use a laptop on a counter so they can move while they think (body movement), provides self-assessments (logic/math), has exercises requiring students to go outside and gather real-world examples (nature), creates interactivity (social), uses audio files for music and voice (language, music), insists on reflection (self), and has well-laid-out images and text (spatial) will encourage multiple approaches to the material. The best approach for instructors is to be aware of the wide variety of developed intelligences and preferred learning methods and to keep that variety in mind when creating course materials and activities. Variety of experience can reduce the distance between the student and the environment of the web, a significant benefit when so much of the learning is done independently.

Creating Engaging Presentations: Reducing Student-Content Distance

Text, images, and multimedia that are loaded into an online course for student viewing are often referred to as the class "content." However, since interactive elements may also be contained within the course, a better term might be "presentation." Presentation elements are designed to be read, seen, or heard by the student. They are considered passive elements that relay information rather than require active involvement. The earliest online classes were almost exclusively presentation, rather like the old correspondence courses by mail. Many still are, reflecting the perpetuation of the classroom-lecturing model in online classes.

Different presentation elements can be used to reach text/language, visual, and spatial learning styles. Textual tone and approach reflect the social presence of the instructor. For this reason, the style of writing for informational material should strike a balance between scholarly detachment (as in a formal lecture) and colloquial communication (as in a personal email). Images should be truly illustrative rather than decorative and be placed near the text they illustrate to support spatial interrelationships.

Multimedia in presentations also access the aural and spatial learning styles of students. Instructor-created audio and video add an important element of individuality and social presence to an online class, where students can often feel distanced from the professor. While a number of colleges have facilities where an instructor can be filmed or recorded during a lecture, it is not difficult to set up a small system in the office, using a microphone, MP3 recorder, or video camera. Free multimedia programs come with most computers or are available free for editing, compressing, and resizing multimedia objects. Multimedia can be linked as files inside the class, embedded in a page, or served as podcasts to which students can subscribe. Quick screencasts can be created, with the instructor's voice leading students through a task or website, perhaps in answer to a student's question. Such methods make it clear that the instructor is "really there."

Audio and video content can, of course, be obtained from many sources other than the instructor. Copyrighted music and video can be used under the guidelines of the TEACH Act (Technology, Education and Copyright Harmonization Act of 2002), and again there is some support for fair use if only enrolled students can access the video. It is possible to digitally convert everything from old record albums to VHS video footage. Video-sharing websites feature a large selection of possible video sources, and some sites even include embedding code so the linked clip can appear directly in a webpage. More and more content providers, such as PBS, are providing instructional videos and clips in many disciplines for free or through institutional subscription.

Another source of media is publisher-created content. A large number of textbooks come with not only CD-ROMs, but also entire websites to which students can subscribe through the bookstore and modules that can upload an entire class of materials directly into a course management system. These packages have advantages and disadvantages. The main advantage is access to a large number of quality materials. The disadvantages include restrictions on transferring content outside the course management system, difficulty selecting only the content needed, and using content from semester to semester without repurchasing the connected textbook. A more serious disadvantage is that publisher packages create canned, cookie-cutter courses that can be taught by anyone and do not contain any of the social presence of the instructor.

When using different approaches for presentation, it is important to recall that not all students have the same ability to access information. Accessibility has become a major issue since the adoption of Section 508 as part of the 1998 amendments to the Rehabilitation Act of 1973. For instructors already accustomed to offering their class elements to support various learning styles, accessibility is rarely a problem. Many of the techniques (providing text as an alternative to images, providing a written transcript of a video clip, using descriptive links) offer a rich learning experience for all students and a chance for all students to succeed in class. Other techniques that are not quite as intuitive make good sense after some thought about the limitations of those who are visually or aurally impaired: not using color as an indicator, using special table coding so that text readers (which read the page aloud in synthesized speech) read the headings of each row or column first. Websites such as W3C's Web Accessibility Initiative (www.w3.org/WAI/) can help instructors make web material accessible for everyone.

Good presentation does not just relay quantities of information. It can reach a number of different learning styles and can be effective in reducing distance, especially if the teacher's voice or face is featured. What presentation cannot do, however, is actively engage the student in either creating an online community or interacting with the material.

Discussion for Learning: Reducing Student-Student Distance

One area where the Net Gen research may be right is the perceived need of students to learn with each other (Oblinger and Oblinger 2005). While some instructors consider discussion to be secondary to presentation, more and more are looking at social interaction as primary to learning, with the goal being an engaged learner (Conrad and Donaldson 2004, 13). The ability of students to construct their own knowledge in concert with others brings several elements into play, including communication standards, development of online community, responsibility toward others, expression and exchange of learned ideas, and public processing of information.

Current research indicates much support for using a highly facilitative teaching style instead of relying on presentation of information. As we have seen, the environment of online learning creates isolation. Students' use of the Internet for social interaction (email, instant messaging, social sites) does not change the basic problem of distance, because web *learning* is not the same as web *use*. The options inherent in ordinary use of the web, such as menus with choices and immediacy of feedback, do not translate into online classes, which tend to have deadlines and expectations (Laird 2003). When the individualized isolation inherent in online learning is added to concern about expectations and evaluation, the result can be loss of interest and confidence on the part of the student. The research, while not yet clear about the improvement of learning achieved by social interaction, is very clear about the importance to student satisfaction and persistence in the course (Berge 2002, 181). Several technologies and approaches allow an instructor to create an environment that reduces distance through student-student interaction.

Asynchronous Discussion

Asynchronous discussion (a discussion board) is a standard feature of many online classes because it provides both social interaction and time-shifting flexibility. It is the place where students decide their level of engagement in the class, whether they feel comfortable, whether they want to continue. Asynchronous discussion posting allows time for thought, since responses do not have to be instantaneous. Time for thought, however, does not necessarily mean that thought will happen. The lag time also can mean that the thread of discussion can be easily lost or that threads can become long and unwieldy. Novice instructors tend to post a question or topic, perhaps weekly, to be answered by students, and demand a certain number of posts or replies. If the question is fairly factual or has only one or two possible answers, the first few students posting will answer the question and the others will simply agree, preventing any critical discourse. In one sense, creating such a closed discussion is like stretching out over a long period that which could have been covered in a few minutes of classroom time (Al-Bataineh, Brooks, and Bassoppo-Moyo 2005, 286). This approach can quickly turn a discussion forum into nothing more than a posting board, where students have no reason to interact.

The instructor's role in an asynchronous discussion should be carefully chosen based on the teaching style. Resources such as *Facilitating Online Learning: Effective Strategies for Moderators* (Collison et al. 2000) can be useful in helping instructors determine the desired approach. If instructor participation is too frequent and corrective, the entire discussion can be shut down (the expert has spoken!). A good starting point would be to consider the instructor as a discussion facilitator, whose job it is to come in occasionally to summarize, guide, and encourage depth. One way to do this is by priming the discussion with open questions, controversial topics, or modules designed to elicit emotion or response. As discussion continues, the instructor can interject with deeper questions, connections, and guidance.

Synchronous Chat

Synchronous chat has many uses in an online class. Instant communication means less alienation, since the conversation is clearly mutual. Some instructors set up free instant messaging accounts (such as Yahoo IM or AOL Instant Messenger) and open the chat window for office hours with individual students. Chat rooms, where instructors can meet with groups of students at the same time, can be found in a number of course management systems and on the Internet (though some of these may be open to everyone and not appropriate for class use). Facilitating a chat requires a different set of skills than facilitating an asynchronous discussion board, because everything is "on the fly." Large groups become unwieldy—small groups of five to ten students tend to work best. The instructor should have a set of goals to achieve in a particular period of time and be willing to start with a bit of social banter so that everyone feels comfortable before diving into more topical concerns. In addition to requiring more skills on the part of the instructor, chat requires students to be at the computer at a particular time, which can undermine the flexibility they expect in an online class.

Videoconferencing

Videoconferencing programs, if available through the institution, can provide an entire synchronous class experience, complete with whiteboard, desktop sharing, voice chat, and text chat. Classes can meet online, live, at a particular time, and participants can hand off the microphone to each other. Instructors interested in this approach should consider attending a few online conferences, many of which now use these technologies for presentation and interactive sessions. These programs create a multitasking environment where text chat, voice, and presentation are all going on simultaneously. They can create an excellent place for community building and group participation.

Constructivist Projects

Constructivist projects can make it easier for social interaction to be part of a task, rather than the objective itself. A wiki (a webpage that can be written and edited by a group) can be used to create class projects or even serve as the site for an entire class. Student-written blogs can be shared and peer evaluated. Even a standard discussion forum can be used to have students construct collections and case studies and work together on analysis. Social bookmarking can be used to have a class or group amass and critique resources.

Large Multiuser Environments

Large multiuser environments, originally based on online games, can create virtual three-dimensional space for interactivity. The largest of such communities is Second Life, a virtual world where instructors can rent land, set up a classroom, and teach an entire class through their own avatar. Such places, while somewhat surreal, have provided extraordinary opportunities for teaching and learning, since structures can be built and spatial concepts explored in a way impossible using only text-based communication.

Personal Learning Environments

Personal learning environments (PLEs) put students in far more control of their own learning than typical online classes. PLEs are sets of tools—which can be determined by the instructor—that students use to construct their own learning experience, creating modules of content and interactivity with colleagues. The syllabus for such a course might consist of access to a tool page (such as Elgg), guidelines for topic construction, and participation in discussions. Students could be assessed on the quality of the construction of their learning environment.

There is an automatic equality that comes from interacting online. Even though the instructor may set up rules and parameters for asynchronous and synchronous communication, there is no way to determine how the discussion will go or who might dominate it. There is no way to be sure that all the instructing is coming from the instructor! Web-based applications provide many opportunities to decentralize learning. Almost any website can be used educationally. For example, a number of professors complain about Wikipedia, an open-content website that students use excessively as a reference. Yet the fact that every Wikipedia entry has a history that can be viewed and tracked provides opportunities for discussing how entries are created. The sharing and tagging of the growing collection of user-uploaded content (videos, bookmarks lists, friends lists, blogs, images) have created opportunities for anyone to learn and anyone to teach. The reduction in isolation and the increase in engagement can be substantial with such methods.

Assessment as Feedback: Further Reducing Distance

Although most people think of formal multiple-choice, short-answer, or essay exams when they hear the word "assessment," tests can also be seen as a further opportunity for learning. Feedback and evaluation have goals beyond assessment and grades, including increasing motivation, linking the goals of the course to real life, and providing information for the instructor to improve the class (Berge 2002, 186). Not all assessments need be graded. In fact, in an online environment, offering only formal assessments can be detrimental. Due to the variety of learning styles and the isolation of the online learning environment, students should be offered a variety of ways to succeed in the course.

Interacting with the content itself is one of three ways students can learn actively online (the other two are interaction with the instructor and interaction with colleagues). Lessons can guide the student through a set of content. In Moodle, for example, it is possible to construct guided paths ("branched lessons") through the material. Answers to questions provided along the way guide students to different pages depending on their responses. Interactive Flash or PowerPoint presentations make it possible for students to interact with the material in a similar way.

Self-assessments, which can be easily created in any course management system or quiz program, provide students an opportunity to test their skill without risking their grade. Automatic feedback can be given through the program. Items requiring similar skills can then be offered in the formal test. To prevent cheating when using a course management system, large pools of test questions are advisable. The program can then vary the set of problems presented in the test, allowing students to take the test more than once, perhaps for an averaged grade. A large pool of test questions can even become a self-assessment or study mechanism in itself!

The distance of the online setting makes it difficult for students to glean what instructors expect and to understand why they are getting the grades they receive. Rubrics or lists of expectations can be used for all evaluative aspects of an online class. Expectations for discussion posts regarding content, not just frequency, should be made clear and modeled by the teacher. Good answers from a recent test can be posted to show levels of quality. Private communications should be welcomed when students have a grading concern.

Instructors should consider offering formative as well as summative assessments. Summative evaluations, which measure student achievement on a scale in terms of points as a grade, are typical—the purpose is accountability. Formative evaluations can let the students know how they are doing as their work progresses. Classroom assessment techniques call for metacognition, the students' own evaluation of how well they are learning, and can be used online. For example, students could be asked to post the most interesting thing they learned and the most confusing concept they encountered from the previous lesson (Angelo and Cross 1993). The results could be collected and shared with everyone.

The Humanities Connection

It should be remembered that the distance between student and instructor is the reason online courses are so popular: students want the convenience of working at varied times and from various locations. Some might also be content with not being involved in their studies, just reading the book and taking tests. But a college education in the humanities requires engagement. The very nature of humanities studies demands social interaction, the sharing of ideals, the collective interaction with people, past and present. Today's technologies allow instructors to create rich experiences in their online classes and ameliorate the isolation inherent in taking a class in a distancing environment.

References

Al-Bataineh, Adel, S. Leanne Brooks, and Temba C. Bassoppo-Moyo. 2005. "Implications of Online Teaching and Learning." *International Journal of Instructional Media* 32, no. 3: 285–294.

Angelo, Thomas A., and Patricia K. Cross. 1993. *Classroom Assessment Techniques: A Handbook for College Teachers*. San Francisco: Jossey-Bass.

Berge, Zane L. 2002. "Active, Interactive, and Reflective eLearning." *Quarterly Review of Distance Education* 3, no. 2: 181–190.

Collison, George, Bonnie Elbaum, Sarah Haavind, and Robert Tinker. 2000. *Facilitating Online Learning: Effective Strategies for Moderators*. Madison, WI: Atwood.

Conrad, Rita-Marie, and J. Ana Donaldson. 2004. *Engaging the Online Learner: Activities and Resources for Creative Instruction.* San Francisco: Jossey-Bass.

Gardner, Howard. 1983. *Frames of Mind: The Theory of Multiple Intelligences.* New York: Basic Books.

Grant, Donna M., Alisha D. Malloy, and Marianne C. Murphy. 2009. "A Comparison of Student Perceptions of Their Computer Skills to Their Actual Abilities." *Journal of Information Technology Education* 8: 141–160.

Joyce, Kristopher M., and Abbie Brawon. 2009. "Enhancing Social Presence in Online Learning: Mediation Strategies Applied to Social Networking Tools." *Online Journal of Distance Learning Administration* 12, no. 4. www.westga.edu/~distance/ojdla/winter124/joyce124.html.

Laird, Ellen. 2003. "I'm Your Teacher, Not Your Internet Service Provider." *Chronicle of Higher Education*, January 3.

Lewis, Cassandra C., and Husein Abdul-Hamid. 2006. "Implementing Effective Online Teaching Practices: Voices of Exemplary Faculty." *Innovative Higher Education* 31, no. 2: 83–98.

Oblinger, Diana G., and James L. Oblinger, eds. 2005. *Educating the Net Generation.* EDUCAUSE. www.educause.edu/educatingthenetgen.

Pashler, Harold, Mark McDaniel, Doug Rohrer, and Robert Bjork. 2009. "Learning Styles: Concepts and Evidence." *Psychological Science in the Public Interest* 9, no. 3: 105–119.

Pedró, Francesc. 2009. "New Millennium Learners in Higher Education: Evidence and Policy Implications." *Technology in Higher Education.* OECD/CERI (September). www.nml-conference.be/wp-content/uploads/2009/09/NML-in-Higher-Education.pdf.

Prensky, Marc. 2001. "Digital Natives, Digital Immigrants." *On the Horizon* 9, no. 5: 1–6.

Smith, Shannon D., Gail Salaway, and Judith Borreson Caruso. 2009. "The ECAR Study of Undergraduate Students and Information Technology, 2009." EDUCAUSE (October). www.educause.edu/Resources/TheECARStudyof UndergraduateStu/187215.

$$\boxed{3}$$

Using Electronic Courseware

Lessons for Educators

Sharmila Pixy Ferris and Maureen C. Minielli

Over the past two decades a range of factors, including the rising costs of higher education and the changing nature of educational institutions, has led the call for a change from the traditional, space-and-time-bound institutions to ones that offer increasingly cost-effective, electronically enhanced programs. From the students' perspective, external demands, including work and family, increased costs of living, and inconvenient class time offerings, are fueling increasing demands for nontraditional means of learning. As institutions of higher education turn to technology, primarily Internet-based, to address these challenges, the use of electronic courseware—or eCourseware—has dramatically increased. Thus this is an opportune moment for an examination of technologically related pedagogical issues. Technologies, particularly online, are currently in a state of high interpretive flexibility (Brent 2005), meaning that such tools are amenable to shaping. This makes a pedagogical focus particularly meaningful and necessary today. In this chapter we consider eCourseware from a pedagogical perspective, with the goal of aiding educators with their effective adoption, implementation, and utilization of technology in teaching and learning.

We begin with a brief discussion of the growth of online education and the technologies it employs before proceeding to a focus on effective teaching. Educators need a basic foundation in order to effectively navigate eCourseware. After a brief survey of terminology, functions, and uses, we proceed to the primary focus of this chapter: some guiding lessons for effective usage of eCourseware. Our goal is to help educators at various levels of technological expertise utilize the courseware to promote effective teaching and learning.

Growing Use of eCourseware

The use of eCourseware has increased dramatically since its introduction well over a decade ago. As Vicky Phillips, founder and CEO of Geteducated.com notes, "online learning has reached mass cultural acceptance. It's no longer the ugly stepsister of the higher-education world" (Breslau 2009). Today eCourseware is used in both traditional and online courses. Its classroom prevalence is evidenced in an EDUCAUSE study that found the penetration of eLearning activities to be 100 percent of surveyed institutions (Arabasz and Baker 2003) and from statistics indicating its rapid growth in face-to-face classrooms: 55 percent in 2009, compared to 50 percent in 2007 and 34 percent in 2003 (Green 2009a). The growth of technology usage in higher education is supported by a sharp increase in the number of students attending school. Online enrollment has increased almost twentyfold in the past seven years and is expected to continue growing at an annual rate of 30 percent, according to the North American Council for Online Learning (Xinhua General News Service 2007).

The growing use of technology in online education is also supported by ongoing data from the Sloan Consortium. Its 2003 and 2004 reports indicated that nearly 96 percent of American institutions of higher education offered online opportunities to over 3.2 million students. In 2009 the Sloan Survey of Online Learning reported that over 4.5 million students were enrolled in at least one online course during the fall 2008 semester, representing a 17 percent increase over the previous year. Specifically, "more than one out of four college and university students now take at least one course online" (Ascribe Newswire 2010), up from one out of ten in 2002 (*PC Magazine* 2009). Kevin Carey, the policy director of Education Sector, puts the online participation rate at 20 percent but notes that nearly one in ten college students take courses solely online, a percentage that is expected to increase (National Public Radio 2009). In many areas of the United States, online enrollment is outpacing traditional enrollment (U.S. State News 2007). As the first decade of the new century draws to a close, the overall growth rate for online education is nearly 13 percent, compared to a nominal 1.2 percent increase for traditional brick-and-mortar classes (State News Service 2009).

The data overwhelmingly demonstrates how the use of technology is reshaping higher education. *PC Magazine* indicates that nearly one-half of the 4,500 brick-and-mortar colleges and universities now offer online degree programs (2009). Online programs at traditional schools, such as the University of Massachusetts and Thomas Edison College, have witnessed 90 percent to 100 percent growth since 2006 (Breslau 2009), while Pennsylvania State University offers a "World Campus" with "an enrollment of 10,000 from 62 countries" (Wilson 2010).

The expansion of electronic learning has paralleled the growth of eCourseware as colleges and universities seek consistent platforms for their course offerings. Today eCourseware products are as common on campus as classroom desks, with one system, Blackboard/WebCT, dominating (with a market share estimate ranging from 57 percent to 66 percent, according to Delta Initiative 2009). In the past decade, eCourseware has become ubiquitous across higher education in three notable ways: as a supplement to the traditional classroom in which the instructor meets the students face-to-face; as the primary platform of online learning or distance education; and as an essential element in the hybrid or blended classroom, which combines the elements of traditional and distance learning (Arabasz and Baker 2003). To promote an understanding of the effective pedagogical use of eCourseware, we briefly define it.

eCourseware Defined

eCourseware is software that is designed for teaching and learning in education and industry. Depending on this software's usage or geographical location, it is variously and commonly called *learning content management systems*, *learning management systems*, and *course management systems*. Other terms such as *collaboration and learning environment* and *virtual learning environments* suggest potential future directions as contemporary products develop to meet educational needs. While these software programs share many features, differences warrant a consideration. We briefly review the three most common (global) iterations of eCourseware in order to provide some choices for those educators who have the luxury of selecting the tools they use for online teaching and learning. As well, such a basic overview can assist in an understanding of the pedagogical lessons we offer later.

Learning Content Management Systems and Learning Management Systems

A learning management system (LMS) is a software system for the creation, storage, management, and usage of learning content. LMSs include "authoring, classroom management, competency management, knowledge management, certification or compliance training, personalization, mentoring, chat and discussion boards" (*Transform* 2003). According to the 2009 Campus Computing Survey, 92 percent of schools utilize a single LMS for their entire campus (Green 2009a).

Course Management Systems

Course management systems (CMSs) currently dominate higher education in the United States. Simonson (2007) defines them as software "designed to assist in the management of educational courses for students, especially by helping teachers and learners with course administration" and tracking of learners' progress. While generally perceived as primary tools for virtual or distance education, CMSs also are used to support the traditional face-to-face and hybrid classrooms (Arabasz and Baker 2003). For educators, CMSs offer a variety of tools, including information management and data management resources, communication and messaging tools, conferencing tools, calendars, syllabi, assessment and grading tools, and student portfolios. There are two predominant types of CMS in use today—open source and commercial.

Open Source CMS

Open Source CMSs are either free or available after payment of a nominal membership fee. One popular international open source CMS is Moodle, an acronym for Modular Object-Oriented Dynamic Learning Environment (Thibodeaux 2006). Moodle is used by over 70,000 institutions globally (Doesburg 2009) with more than 330,000 registered users (Ellis 2009). Moodle's popularity has steadily grown in the latter half of the new century's decade, growing from 4.2 percent in 2006 to 7.8 percent in 2007 (Young 2008). Moodle is useful to educators because, unlike comparable programs, it operates on a variety of platforms, including Linux, Windows, Mac, and Netware (Timson 2007).

Another growing open source CMS is the Sakai Project, which initially combined the best tools and solutions from CMSs created at four U.S. universities: Indiana University, Massachusetts Institute of Technology, University of Michigan, and Stanford University. Sakai Project operates like an open-source program, but it does charge an access fee for source code—the relatively modest fee of $10,000 for schools with enrollment over 3,000, and $5,000 for those institutions with enrollment under 3,000 (see Sakaiproject.org). Today nearly 200 institutions from the United States and globally utilize the Sakai program (PR Newswire 2010).

Commercial CMS

Commercial CMSs consist of fee-based instructional technology packages purchased by institutions of higher education. Proprietary CMSs are primarily distinguished from open-source systems by their cost, which can be substantial. The most widely used commercial CMSs in the United States are Blackboard (www.blackboard.com, now merged with WebCT), eCollege (www.ecollege.com), and Desire2Learn (www.desire2learn). Perhaps foreshadowing a future merger of open and commercial CMSs, the 2009 release of Blackboard 9.0 now allows for the seamless integration of open CMSs like Moodle and Sakai within its system (Associated Press Financial Wire 2009).

Whatever the type of eCourseware, a number of common features exist for educators. Tools include information management and data resources, communication and messaging tools, conferencing tools, assessment tools, and others. Information management and data resources include options such as file exchange, editing, web browsing, and whiteboards (with image and PowerPoint functions). Messaging tools include Chat, email, and threaded discussions, with posts possible in plain text, formatted text, or html, with attachments and URLs. Message management includes viewing of threaded discussions by date and by thread, and archiving. Conferencing tools include synchronous tools such as Chat and internal small groups with their own whiteboards, discussion forums, and synchronous and asynchronous communication tools. Other functions associated with teaching are also included—such as gradebooks, assessment tools, tools for creation and archiving of course content, and web links.

Various industry leaders are expanding offerings to make their systems more attractive. For example, Blackboard has partnered with NBC News to deliver its media content to users and offers instant messaging and access to iTunes U (PR Newswire 2009a, 2009b, 2009c). The eCourseware providers are also working with the current trend toward mobility, so students can access tools through devices like smart phones. For example, Blackboard has announced smart phone applications (M2 Presswire 2009; Schaffhauser 2009), but also has expanded its mobility reach by including course information accessibility on the Bing web browser and enhanced student identification verification (PR Newswire 2009d, 2009e); the Sakai Project released its own mobility application in fall 2009 (States News Service 2009), and Desire2Learn is embracing the mobility trend with its recent announcement of a partnership with RIM (Research in Motion) to release Desire2Learn2Go (TendersInfo 2009). The trends toward increased ease of mobile learning have significant implications for educators, as we will discuss later.

Whether commercial or open source, the range and selection of eCourseware services and tools offer abundant teaching opportunities for educators. As Riddiford (2009) points out, educational institutions are responding, with nearly 60 percent of American college and university leaders currently considering online education as "critical to their long-term strategies."

eCourseware and Pedagogy

Courseware vendors, as could be expected, sing the pedagogical benefits of their software. For instance, former WebCT CEO Carol Vallone has said that her company's eCourseware led to "improved learning, higher retention and graduation rates, more efficient use of classroom capacity, and increased revenue through new instructional programs for an expanded enrollment of students" (Warger 2003). While such praise can be discounted from those who stand to gain financially, academics echo the support of eCourseware. Katz (2003), for example, lauds CMSs as an "essential step in the evolution of the academy," stating that the development and use of CMSs "over time, will promote both access to post-secondary instruction and learning itself." The influential Peter Drucker predicted that "postsecondary education would either be delivered by technology, through the Internet, or become wastelands" (cited in Kanuka 2006).

Such claims appear to put the technology before pedagogy. We feel strongly that educators using eCourseware must remember, first, that pedagogy should drive technology and, second, that issues of teaching and learning are of ultimate importance to students and teachers. Once instructors recognize these important facts, then they can understand how technology changes the way they teach and that eCourseware requires them to work toward changes in traditional methods of teaching and learning. To this end, we offer seven pedagogical lessons for users of eCourseware, whether in the online classroom, as supplements to the traditional classroom, or in the hybrid, blended classroom. Building on our own eCourseware experiences as well as a wide range of research, our seven lessons also promote Chickering and Gamson's (1987) classic principles of good education. These principles have guided pedagogy for more than two decades. In summary, they state that good teaching (1) encourages contact between students and faculty; (2) develops reciprocity and cooperation among students; (3) encourages active learning; (4) gives prompt feedback; (5) emphasizes time on task; (6) communicates high expectations; and (7) respects diverse talents and ways of learning.

Lesson #1: New Avenues for Teaching and Learning

While it may appear a truism today, the ability of eCourseware to span space and time provides the first lesson for educators. The ability of technology to transcend the barriers of time and space opens new avenues for teaching and learning by allowing students flexible, mobile access to learning systems and enables learning to occur anywhere and anytime. Not only is flexibility possible in access to information systems (libraries, databases, and tutorials), but so is contact with educators, experts, and peers, locally and across vast geographical distances.

Flexibility in time and space is an invaluable benefit of eCourseware. Escaping the rule-bound, time-bound nature of the traditional classroom can stimulate student engagement and involvement. eCourseware also affords self-paced learning, utilizing a wide range of eCourseware services such as access to course and lecture notes, file sharing, collaborative editing, anytime-anyplace contact with teacher and classmates, and whiteboards. Access to lecture notes, written and oral (through podcasting and vodcasting), is particularly noteworthy as this was a resource not easily available to students in the pre-eCourseware classroom. Even if instructors do not post lecture and study material, students generally have durable access to content that supplements their textbook.

Engaging students in learning, whether through such eCourseware features as flexible learning and access to notes, or through eCourseware's means of teaching to diverse learning styles, is a compelling way to improve student learning. Recent research shows that engagement has a significant positive impact on student success (NSSE 2006).

While eCourseware offers many new avenues for teaching and learning, in considering changes in pedagogy educators must also have an understanding of the challenges faced by contemporary students. Learning "anywhere and anytime" is challenged by a range of factors including a greater need to work outside of college, financial problems exacerbated by rising costs, lack of college readiness, and differences in learning styles (Kuh 2007). In addition, educators must contend with issues of student isolation engendered by the constraints of technology (O'Neill, Singh, and O'Donoghue 2004).

These complex and sometimes conflicting factors require that educators recognize and accept the greater demands of learning with eCourseware by designing engaging alternative learning environments. The following lessons offer more information on some ways to do so.

Lesson #2: From Traditional Purveyors of Knowledge to Facilitators of Learning

An immediate effect of Lesson #1 makes itself felt in the traditional role of teacher as purveyor of knowledge. The use of eCourseware allows students to access a staggering amount of information on an ongoing basis. Computer storage systems, databases, and the Internet remove the need for the traditional focus on high-quality, text-based knowledge, as educators are recognizing. A comprehensive survey of educators by the National Education Association found that a majority agreed that quality of information was higher with electronic resources (2000).

eCourseware technology also provides quick and painless access to information through the Internet. Students have access to a world of knowledge, including factual information from every discipline, and multimedia artifacts from film and audio recordings to art and cultural artifacts. Not only does this availability to resources radically change the structure of the traditional classroom, but also it constrains educators to adapt to new roles since they no longer need to function as the sole repository of expert knowledge in the classroom. Many teachers find this particular lesson hard, as they come from a millennium-long tradition of educator-as-didactic-authority. But the success of moving to a new role as *facilitator* rather than purveyor of information can be seen in MIT's Comparative Media Studies program, which recognizes the need for a new style of teaching. Rather than traditional classes taught by one teacher, this program has a "pool of loosely affiliated faculty members who participate in an ad hoc manner" to meet student interests. The faculty pool is not limited to the departmental or program members, but can be drawn from other universities, or industry, internationally (Jenkins 2007). MIT's program truly allows teachers to be facilitators of knowledge, providing expertise when and where needed.

If educators are willing to relinquish some of the power than goes with the controlling, didactic, traditional teaching method, students using eCourseware will benefit through guided access to a world of information. But for effective learning, students continue to need a guiding hand from educators in critically evaluating information, which leads us to the next lesson.

Lesson #3: From Content to Critical Thinking and Evaluation

The educator's changing role to facilitator of knowledge is the most obvious change imposed by eCourseware (as students can potentially obtain a much wider range of knowledge through the use of technology than the individual educator could provide), yet the sheer amount of information available on the web creates its own problems for students. As many educators have lamented, the ability to acquire information does not bring with it the ability to critically evaluate or effectively utilize that information. Students' lack of critical thinking is an ongoing problem, as was pointed out before the advent of the Internet by Neil Postman (Postman 1992), and continues to be noted today by many educators. The importance of critical thinking in the classroom is reinforced by most national accrediting institutions such as Middle States (www.msche.org), and organizations such as the American Library Association (www.ala.org/ala/acrl/acrlissues/acrlinfolit/infolitoverview/introtoinfolit/introinfolit.cfm) and the American Association of State Colleges and Universities (www.aascu.org) to name a few. Thus it is clear that in higher education today the educator's role is seen as extending beyond that of providing prescriptive knowledge to a larger focus on the continued development of critical thinking skills.

It thus behooves educators to understand not only *how* to effectively facilitate students' search for, and consumption of, appropriate and relevant information, but how to *guide* them in understanding and analyzing that information. Beyond simply guiding their search for knowledge and understanding, instructors must endeavor to teach critical thinking skills through the tools provided by eCourseware.

It is a benefit of the asynchronous aspects of eCourseware that students' critical thinking skills can be supported with increased time for reflection and evaluation of content, without disruption of continuity in learning. Both synchronous and asynchronous forms of computer-mediated technologies allow for extended discussions and learning transactions outside the classroom and for increased peer-to-peer dialogue—factors that promote analysis and problem-solving and thus critical thinking. Additionally, as Chickering and Ehrmann (1996) observe, "significant real-life problems, conflicting perspectives, or paradoxical data sets can set powerful learning challenges that drive students to not only acquire information but sharpen their cognitive skills of analysis, synthesis, application, and evaluation."

The distanced and asynchronous nature of learning through eCourseware promotes another aspect of critical thinking: learning how to manage time effectively. Chickering and Ehrmann (1996) feel that "allocating realistic amounts of time means effective learning for students and effective teaching for faculty." It is their opinion that technology can "improve time on task for students and faculty members" as well as making studying more efficient. In this manner, eCourseware not only promotes critical thinking skills, but also advances Chickering and Gamson's (1987) fifth principle of good practice—emphasizing time on task. It also allows for the sixth principle of good practice, the communication of high expectations. Technology allows faculty to "communicate high expectations explicitly and efficiently" (Chickering and Ehrmann 1996).

Improved critical thinking skills are undeniably associated with more effective learning. But to more successfully move students beyond content-based learning to the development of higher-order cognitive skills, educators need to move beyond traditional instructional methods.

Lesson #4: From Traditional to New Instructional Design

As educators learn to modify their roles to facilitators rather than purveyors of knowledge and as they learn to guide students to seek, understand, and analyze information, it becomes clear that the use of eCourseware requires educators to develop new methods of instructional design and pedagogy. Advice from Lee and Reigeluth (1994) almost two decades ago still holds true: teachers must "develop new educational agenda . . . change the content of traditional curricula, reorder the curriculum based on a new array of skills . . . and change the style of classroom instruction." Yet little has changed in the decades since they made their plea.

Seven years after Lee and Reigeluth's article was published, a major Pew study found that the vast majority of online courses are taught in the same manner as their traditional equivalents. They are organized in much the same manner as are their campus counterparts: developed by individual faculty members, with some support from the IT staff, and offered within a semester or quarter framework. Most follow traditional academic practices ("Here's the syllabus, go off and read or do research, come back and discuss"), and most are evaluated using traditional student-satisfaction methods (Twigg 2001).

Educators' refusal to change their teaching seems shortsighted. Methods of innovative, yet sound instructional design abound today. Some of these methods are clearly facilitated by eCourseware, such as the use of multimedia and computer-based instruction like tutorials, drills, and online assessments with immediate feedback. Other innovative pedagogical methods are independent of eCourseware but work well with it. Such methods include, but are not by any means limited to, collaborative learning, project-oriented teaching, problem-based learning, and computer-mediated communication tools like simulations, blogs, and wikis. While all these methods differ widely, they share a focus on active learning, thus promoting Chickering and Gamson's (1987) third principle of good practice.

In learning and adapting their teaching methods to best employ technology, educators should also take into account Chickering and Gamson's (1987) seventh principle of good practice: respecting students' diverse talents and ways of learning. This is facilitated by eCourseware, which allows students to learn at their own pace, through direct learning or virtual experiences, aurally and visually, self-reflection, problem solving, and structured and open-ended assignments (Chickering and Ehrmann 1996).

A wide range of pedagogical options is available as instructors work to develop new methods of instruction, but the important point is that curricula be revised to include those methods that take advantage of, and effectively work with, eCourseware technologies.

Lesson #5: Rethinking Communication and Relationships With Students

Moving away from technology to pedagogy while keeping a focus on learning and student issues leads us to another area in which educators must learn from CMSs—to rethink traditional communication with students and, correspondingly, rethink interpersonal relationships. The communication technologies of CMSs greatly facilitate quantity and (theoretically) quality of communication, allowing for greater interactivity between students and instructors. They extend the boundaries of the classroom physically and temporally, extend and stimulate discussions, and allow for the continuation of dialogue outside the classroom. eCourseware thus compels instructors to communicate with students in ways that extend beyond the traditional.

In extending the means for faculty-student communication, eCourseware promotes two of Chickering and Gamson's (1987) principles of good practice: their first principle of encouragement of contact between students and faculty, and their fourth principle of giving prompt feedback. eCourseware encourages faculty-student contact through its provision of painless means of communication. As Chickering and Ehrmann (1996) note, "technologies can strengthen faculty interactions with all students." They also find that asynchronous communication has been very notably successful in increasing the total amount of faculty-student communication and that many students find this communication satisfyingly "intimate, protected, and convenient." eCourseware also provides several means for faculty to provide feedback to students: through email, in chat rooms, in threaded discussions, by online assessment of assignments through a dropbox, and several other means noted by Chickering and Ehrmann (1996), such as the use of e-portfolios to critique and assess on an ongoing basis "performances that are time-consuming and expensive to record and evaluate—such as leadership skills, group process management, or multicultural interactions."

These issues lead to dual and somewhat dichotomous outcomes. On the one hand, the educator must deal with modification of the traditional student-teacher relationship by becoming more accessible to students. On the other hand, these changes in communication and interpersonal relationships encourage flexibility of roles, remove boundaries, and reduce the power differential in the classroom (at least notionally). The "electronic distance" of the medium can lead to reduction of social distance and change the dynamics of the student-teacher relationship, while the accessibility of the teacher is promoted through 24/7 email. Many educators find themselves uncomfortable with these new conditions, but they must consider both positive and negative communication issues in order to effectively promote teaching and learning through eCourseware.

Although increased communication opportunities have both benefits and shortcomings, a related unalloyed benefit is increased opportunities for collaboration.

Lesson #6: Increased Opportunities for Collaboration

eCourseware abounds in opportunities for collaborative teaching and learning. For students, eCourseware facilitates Chickering and Gamson's (1987) second principle of good practice, the development of reciprocity and cooperation. eCourseware technology offers unique and unparalleled opportunities for collaborative student learning, from wikis (open-editing sites) to blogs (journaling sites) to group projects. Beyond these newer applications, technology also facilitates traditional collaborative activities such as "study groups, collaborative learning, group problem solving, and discussion of assignments" (Chickering and Ehrmann 1996).

For faculty, eCourseware offers opportunities to improve teaching by networking with colleagues through scholarly discussion lists, interactive chat, or asynchronous email, thus concomitantly developing professional skills. Access to the web provides global hypertext publication facilities, allowing educators another avenue to share information and learn from each other. The ePortfolio functions of such CMSs as BlackBoard and WebCT provide an easy means to store and transfer information, both text-based and multimedia.

Both students and educators can benefit from collaborative teaching opportunities. Educators can team-teach with colleagues at different universities and even across continents, providing students unique opportunities to interact with peers across different cultures. Some successful examples of collaborative learning can be seen on the individual level, as in the ePALS Classroom Exchange project (www.epals.org), where collaboration can exist synchronously or asynchronously (see Ferris and Wilder 2006), or institutionally. Examples of institutional collaboration can be seen in the Global Classroom Project, linking American, Russian, and NIS (newly independent states) universities together (reported by the Georgia Institute of Technology), and the *Professeurs pour la liberté* program, a Canadian-led collaborative initiative that offers free online education to Africans through the donation of courses from academic institutions from the G8, European, and Scandinavian countries, along with volunteers, books, and reusable computers (Kanuka 2006).

These are also examples of how eCourseware can collaboratively link the classroom to the "real world," allowing educators to develop a project-oriented focus in their instruction. Students and teachers can access a wide range of resources, from their local community to national or global communities, from colleagues and professional organizations to nonprofits and industry. Students can access these resources globally on the Internet, link with their peers, and write for real audiences on the web. Such opportunities can have positive results in the real world, as students extend the collaborative skills learned in the classroom to projects with real impact on the public good (see Ferris 2010).

These increased opportunities for collaborative learning enrich students' learning experiences and also offer educators unique opportunities.

Lesson #7: Educators as Learners

As is evident in Lessons #1 to #6, the effective use of eCourseware requires instructors not only to develop new, student-oriented instructional methods in order to engage them in independent and active learning through and with technology, but also to take a more active and interactive role in the teaching process.

As educators seek a more active role in teaching and learning, they are forced to seize the initiative in becoming leaders in the use and evaluation of eCourseware in the classroom. The need for such pedagogical investigation is underscored by rapid and ongoing changes in students' knowledge of technologies, the extent of which can be seen in a Kaiser Family Foundation study that found that eight- to eighteen-year-olds were prodigious and educated consumers of all forms of media and technology, old and new (2005). As such, students currently entering college as part of the "Net Generation" have unique characteristics with which instructors need to become familiar. For example, such students are technologically savvy, consistent multitaskers who seek instant gratification in the classroom, need independence and involvement in the learning process, and report being bored in the traditional classroom (Barnes, Marateo, and Ferris 2007). Educators need to learn how to harness this generation's love of learning through the use of pedagogical strategies that include meeting them on their own ground: media and technology.

The implication here is that educators must understand the technologies that their students use and must keep up with the rapid and continuing changes. This requires a real and ongoing commitment to learning, as well as time commitment that many instructors are hard-pressed to make. But educators should be able to ask of themselves what they expect from their students. This final lesson may be the hardest, but most important, as they improve their own teaching through the processes of learning.

Institutional Focus and Role

Thus far, our discussion of the effective use of eCourseware has focused on the individual educator. While it is indeed the instructors who bear the largest burden when teaching with eCourseware, they cannot be successful without institutional support. To some extent this support exists; as the use of eCourseware has grown, institutions of higher education have devoted more attention to increasing their own effectiveness. In fact, eCourseware is one of the top ten issues for chief information officers at educational institutions (Camp and DeBlois 2007), but institutional concern with courseware has largely been a concern with technology rather than pedagogy. The Campus Computing Project's 2009 Top Ten list of issues confronting online education in the next few years acknowledges the necessity of pedagogical attention, but the list's major focus is tech-related concerns, including increased demand, internal organization, assessment, Americans with Disabilities Act compliance, and keeping pace with emerging technologies (Green 2009b). This is understandable given that implementation of technology is a necessary precondition to teaching with eCourseware. What is not understandable is a continuing failure to focus equally on the importance of pedagogy. To faculty and student users, the pedagogy is of primary importance—as a landmark Pew study found a decade ago—and remains problematic today (Twigg 2001).

Although institutional focus on pedagogy needs development, there has been an abundance of individual research on courseware and pedagogy. Most of it focuses on the applications of the different types of CMSs. For example, interested readers can learn about the eclectic, growing uses of CMSs in instruction (Christie and Jurado 2009; Fletcher and Cambre 2009) or read a range of research on issues with online pedagogy (Chick and Hassel 2009; Cunningham 2009; Gulati 2008).

For those interested in further reading on institutional roles, we note the pivotal role played by two nonprofit educational institutions in promoting research on teaching with technology and eCourseware. EDUCAUSE (www.educause.edu), whose mission is to "advance higher education by promoting the intelligent use of information technology," has been a pioneer in encouraging research and publication on teaching with courseware, with a range of easily accessible research (www.educause.edu/Resources/Browse/ELearning/17176), while TLT's Flashlight project (www.tltgroup.org) has also long been a resource for educators seeking to improve their teaching through technology.

For faculty and students to more effectively utilize eCourseware, institutions of higher education must also make a commitment to engage in and promote pedagogical effectiveness in teaching and learning with technology.

Conclusion

As instructors utilize eCourseware, both in the virtual classroom and as a supplement to the traditional classroom, they should remember that though it provides a new and exciting tool, with extensive potential, in their teaching repertoire, it is not the only tool, nor should it become their single-minded focus. Their primary concern should remain teaching and learning, and, in considering teaching and learning with technology, instructors must look beyond issues of technology to broader issues of learning. Their goals as educators must include engaging students in higher-order learning, facilitating the exercise of critical thinking skills, and ensuring students' mastery of conceptual, analytical, and theoretical knowledge, as well as, rather than solely, developing students' ability and comfort with the use of technologies.

Although our focus in this chapter has been on lessons for individual educators, we have noted our conviction that individual pedagogical goals cannot be realized without institutional support and commitment. Not only must the institutional infrastructure smoothly maintain the software, but also institutional policies must be appropriate, and technical support must be available to faculty and students (Leacock 2005). Chickering and Ehrmann (1996) best summarize the pivotal role of the institution. Institutional policies concerning learning resources and technology support need to give high priority to user-friendly hardware, software, and communication vehicles that help faculty and students use technologies efficiently and effectively. Investments in professional development for faculty members, plus training and computer lab assistance for students, will be necessary if learning potentials are to be realized.

When strong individual pedagogy meets an enlightened institution, not only do teachers and learners benefit from the promotion of Chickering and Gamson's (1987) principles of good practice, but also the institution benefits in concrete ways. Decreased costs and increased retention are just some of these benefits, as found by the National Center for Academic Transformation. Its director, Carol Twigg, states that more than thirty institutions that have engaged in pedagogical commitments to transforming electronic learning have gained "better grades, fewer class dropouts and lower costs . . . with none doing worse than before the redesign" (Twigg and Graves 2006; complete data available at www.center.rpi.edu).

In closing, we note that it is important that educators consider *now* the effective use of the new technologies afforded by eCourseware or they will find themselves only too rapidly outpaced by the technology itself. A rethinking of traditional teaching and learning is necessary if educators are to effectively utilize eCourseware to make the technological revolution in education meaningful.

Note

An earlier version of this chapter appeared in *First Monday* 10, no. 9 (2005).

References

Arabasz, Paul, and Mary Beth Baker. 2003. *Evolving Campus Support Models for E-learning Courses: ECAR Respondent Summary.* EDUCAUSE Center for Applied Research, March. www.oclc.org/community/topics/elearning/bestpractices/default.htm.

Ascribe Newswire. 2010. "Study: Online Education Up 17 Percent to 4.6 Million; Annual Survey Shows Recession, Influenza Among Factors Driving Growth." January 26. LexisNexis.

Associated Press Financial Wire. 2009. "Blackboard Launches More Open, Flexible Learning Platform Emphasizing Greater Engagement of Students." January 27. LexisNexis.

Barnes, Kassandra, Raymond Marateo, and Sharmila Pixy Ferris. 2007. "Teaching and Learning with the Net Generation." *Innovate* 3, no. 4. www.innovateonline.info.

Brent, Doug. 2005. "Teaching as Performance in the Electronic Classroom." *First Monday* 10, no. 4. http://firstmonday.org/issues/issue10_4/brent/.

Breslau, Karen. 2009. "The Sound of One Hand Clicking; Online Schools Are Booming, Thanks to Their Convenience, Low Cost, and Improved Quality." *Newsweek Kaplan College Guide.* August 17. LexisNexis.

Camp, John S., Peter S. DeBlois, and EDUCAUSE Current Issues Committee. 2007. *Current Issues Survey Report* 30. www.educause.edu/apps/eq/eqm07/eqm0723.asp?bhjs=0andbhrf=http%3A%2F%2Fwww%2Egoogle%2Ecom%2Fsearch%3Fhl%3Den%26ie%3DISO%2D8859%2D1%26q%3Deducause%2B2007%2Bcio%2Bsurvey%26btnG%3DGoogle%2BSearch.

Chick, Nancy, and Holly Hassel. 2009. "'Don't Hate Me Because I'm Virtual': Feminist Pedagogy in the Online Classroom." *Feminist Teacher*, November 3, 195–215. ProjectMUSE.

Chickering, Arthur W., and Stephen C. Ehrmann. 1996. "Implementing the Seven Principles: Technology as Lever." *AAHE Bulletin* (October): 3–6. www.tltgroup. org/programs/seven.html.

Chickering, Arthur W., and Zelda Gamson. 1987. "Seven Principles of Good Practice in Undergraduate Education." Originally published in *AAHE Bulletin*. http://honolulu. hawaii.edu/intranet/committees/FacDevCom/guidebk/teachtip/7princip.htm.

Christie, Michael, and Ramon Garrote Jurado. 2009. "Barriers to Innovation in Online Pedagogy." *European Journal of Engineering Education* 34 (June): 273–279. EBSCOhost.

Cunningham, Craig A. 2009. "Transforming Schooling Through Technology: Twenty-First-Century Approaches to Participatory Learning." *Education and Culture* 25 (November): 46–61. ProjectMUSE.

Delta Initiative. 2009. "State of LMS in Higher Education: Understanding the Big Picture." October. www.slideshare.net/WCETConference/lms-webinar-20091022.

Doesburg, Anthony. 2009. "Catalyst for Change Wins Kudos Abroad." *New Zealand Herald*, December 14. LexisNexis.

Ellis, Ryann K. 2009. "A Field Guide to Learning Management Systems." www. astd.org/NR/rdonlyres/12ECDB99-3B91-403E-9B15-7E597444645D/23395/ LMS_fieldguide_20091.pdf.

Ferris, Sharmila Pixy. 2010. "Potentials for Social Networking and the Public Good." In *Adolescent Online Social Communication and Behavior: Relationship Formation on the Internet*, ed. Robert Zheng, Jason Burrow-Sanchez, and Clifford J. Drew, 167–182 Hershey, PA: IGI Global.

Ferris, Sharmila Pixy, and Hilary Wilder. 2006. "Uses and Potentials of Wikis in Education." *Innovate* 2, no 5. www.innovateonline.info.

Fletcher, Christopher, and Carolina Cambre. 2009. "Digital Storytelling and Implicated Scholarship in the Classroom." *Journal of Canadian Studies* 43 (Winter): 109–130. ProjectMUSE.

Green, Kenneth C. 2009a. "LMS 3.0." *Inside Higher Ed*, November 4. www.insidehighered.com/views/2009/11/04/green.

———. 2009b. "Managing Online Education Programs." October 22. www. campuscomputing.net/sites/www.campuscomputing.net/files/Green-Managing Online%20Ed-Handout.pdf.

Gulati, Shalkni. 2008. "Compulsory Participation in Online Discussion: Is This Constructivism or Normalisation of Learning." *Innovations in Education and Technology* 45 (May): 183–192. ProjectMUSE.

Jenkins, Henry. 2007. "From YouTube to YouNiversity." *Chronicle of Higher Education*, February 16. http://chronicle.com/weekly/v53/i24/24b00901.htm.

Kaiser Family Foundation. 2005. "Generation M: Media in the Lives of 8–18 Year-Olds." www.kff.org/entmedia/entmedia030905pkg.cfm.

Kanuka, Heather. 2006. "Has eLearning Revolutionized Education?" *Embassy: Canada's Foreign Policy Newsletter*, February 26. www.embassymag.ca/html/ index.php?display=storyandfull_path=/2006/february/22/elearning.

Katz, Richard N. 2003. "Balancing Technology and Tradition: The Example of Course Management Systems." *EDUCAUSE Review* 38: 12. www.appa.org/ files/pdfs/03-katz.pdf.

Kuh, George. 2007. "How to Help Students Achieve." *Chronicle of Higher Education*, June 15.

Leacock, Tracy. 2005. "Building a Sustainable e-Learning Development Culture." *Learning Organization* 12: 355–368.

Lee, In-Sook, and Charles M. Reigeluth. 1994. "Empowering Teachers for New Roles in a New Educational System." *Educational Technology* 34: 61–72.

M2 Presswire. 2009. "Blackboard, Inc.: Blackboard Adds iPhone and Mobile Web Platform to Product Suite; Blackboard Acquires Terribly Clever to Support Mobile Education." July 23. LexisNexis.

National Education Association. 2000. "A Survey of Traditional and Distance Learning Higher Education Members." www2.nea.org/he/abouthe/dlstudy.pdf.

National Public Radio. 2009. "Getting an Education on the Internet." September 22. LexisNexis.

National Survey of Student Engagement. 2006. "Engaged Learning: Fostering Success for All Students." *Annual Report*. http://nsse.iub.edu/NSSE_2006_Annual_Report/docs/NSSE_2006_Annual_Report.pdf.

O'Neill, Kayte, Gurmak Singh, and John O'Donoghue. 2004. "Implementing eLearning Programmes for Higher Education: A Literature Review." *Journal of Information Technology Education* 3: 313–323.

PC Magazine. 2009. "Are Online Classes the Future of Learning?" October 1. LexisNexis.

Postman, Neil. 1992. *Technopoly: The Surrender of Culture to Technology*. New York: Knopf.

PR Newswire. 2009a. "Blackboard Adds Multimedia Content from NBC News to the Blackboard Learn Platform; Digital Content and Supplemental Resources Help Bring Courses to Life." October 8. LexisNexis.

———. 2009b. "Blackboard Launches Instant Messaging Within Blackboard Learn(TM); Wimba Pronto(TM) Basic Now Available in the Blackboard Learn Platform." April 2. LexisNexis.

———. 2009c. "Blackboard and Vanderbilt University Partner on iTunes U Integration for Blackboard Learn; Faculty, Students Can Access Multimedia Content Within Their Existing Online Courses." July 15. LexisNexis.

———. 2009d. "Blackboard Joins Forces with Microsoft to Make Course Information Available on Web Browsers; Companies Collaborate on Blackboard Learn for Bing." November 4. LexisNexis.

———. 2009e. "National K-20 Leadership Group Proposes New Model of Student Progression, Highlights Dual Enrollment; Blackboard Establishes Institute to Gather, Share Practice-Driven Guidance for Education Leaders." September 1. LexisNexis.

———. 2010. "Marist's Baron Elected Chair of Sakai Foundation Board." January 18. LexisNexis.

Riddiford, Mike. 2009. "Internet Learning Rebounds." *Australian*, August 26. LexisNexis.

Schaffhauser, Dian. 2009. "Blackboard Adds Blackberry App for Mobile Web Platform." *THE Journal*, November 9. http://thejournal.com/articles/2009/11/09/blackboard-adds-blackberry-app for-mobile-web-platform.aspx?sc_lang=en.

Simonson, Michael. 2007. "Course Management Systems." *Quarterly Review of Distance Education* 8: vii–ix.

Sloan Consortium. 2003. "Sizing the Opportunity: The Quality and Extent of Online Education in the United States, 2002 and 2003." www.sloan-c.org/resources/survey.asp.

———. 2004. "Entering the Mainstream: The Quality and Extent of Online Education in the United States, 2003 and 2004." www.sloanconsortium.org/publications/freedownloads.

State News Service. 2009. "Wanted: iPhone Apps and Soft Skills." December 6. LexisNexis.

TendersInfo. 2009. "Students Going Mobile with Desire2Learn2Go." *TendersInfo*, December 30. LexisNexis.

Thibodeaux, Anna. 2006. "Madison Schools Get Connected With Moodle's Virtual Classroom." *Huntsville Times (Alabama)*, December 20. LexisNexis.

Timson, Lia. 2007. "Using Your Moodle to Deliver Lesson." *The Age*, April 24. LexisNexis.

Transform. 2003. "Find an Answer in E-learning." February: 26–27.

Twigg, Carol A. 2001. "Innovations in Online Learning: Moving Beyond No Significant Difference." www.center.rpi.edu/PewSym/Mon04.html.

Twigg, Carol A., and William H Graves. 2006. "The Future of Course Design and the National Center for Academic Transformation: An Interview with Carol Twigg." *Innovate* 2, no. 3. http://innovateonline.info/index.php?view=articleandid=218.

U.S. State News. 2007. "Spring Webcampus Enrollment Sets Record." February 13. LexisNexis.

Warger, Tom. 2003. "Calling All Course Management Systems." *University Business* 6: 64–65.

Wilson, David. 2010. "How Fine Is Online? The Education Issue." *The Age*, January 30. LexisNexis.

Xinhua General News Service. 2007. "Online Classes Gain Momentum in US." February 4. LexisNexis.

Young, Jeffrey R. 2008. "Blackboard Customers Consider Alternatives." *Chronicle of Higher Education*, September 12. EBSCOhost.

4

Making Course Management Systems Work

Lisa M. Lane

While no carpenter would let the tools in the toolbox (screwdriver, saw, tape measure) determine what should be built, this approach often happens with course management systems (CMSs).[1] CMS, also called learning management system (LMS), is a program or software package designed to serve, present, or host online classes. CMSs vary widely in their features and purpose. Some, like Blackboard and WebCT (now merged into one company), are very large corporate products based on proprietary code; they are often called integrated systems because they combine features such as a gradebook, course materials, and interactive functions into one package. Others, based on open source code, tend to emphasize constructivist learning models while providing various levels of integration. Understanding the pedagogical implications, structural choices, and usage possibilities of such systems can help faculty members create more effective online classes.

Although integrated CMSs vary widely, they all have similar conveniences and challenges for teachers of the humanities. All can be used without knowing much, if anything, about computer code. All focus on organizing and delivering a course in one interface, allow limited customization, and encourage the user to enter information directly into the system (where it is difficult to retrieve). A CMS is not required to create an online class. The challenges of depending on a CMS have led some instructors away from integrated systems and into a more hybrid, mix-and-match approach. The ever-increasing availability of web-based applications means that it is possible to piece together a varied, interactive course without using a CMS at all. Entire courses can be created using a free blog as the foundation.

Some teachers prefer to offer personal learning environments where students (usually referred to as "learners" in such environments) can collaboratively develop their own content and knowledge, an approach pioneered by learning experts like George Siemens (2004) and Stephen Downes (2005). SUNY's Michael Feldstein proposes that "mash-ups" of various web applications should be the foundation of better LMSs (2006).

So why use a CMS at all? Many faculty members have no choice: the institution mandates the use of the system. Even if not required, technical support is far more likely to be available with the institution's chosen CMS. The more innovative approaches may not be appropriate for those new to web technology because they require a great deal of independence on the part of the instructor. However, it is still possible (and desirable) for instructors to manage a standard system in such a way as to achieve their pedagogical goals.

Course Management Versus Learning Management

Although they are often used interchangeably, the terms *course management system* and *learning management system* indicate differing perspectives within the education community. Course management implies an administrative perspective, emphasizing functions such as record-keeping, file storage, and content organization. Learning management implies that the instructor is using the system to enable or monitor learning that is achieved by the student.

Regardless of the designation, studies indicate that such systems are primarily used for administrative purposes rather than improving learning. Faculty members consistently consider the management aspect as primary in their use of a CMS. A University of Wisconsin study showed that although instructors said they adopted a CMS for pedagogical needs, they actually used it for class management: student communication, class documents, and the gradebook (Gastfriend 2005; Morgan 2003). Although one might assume that such limited use applies only to "newbies," a recent study reported that even among experienced online instructors, all commonly used features were purely administrative (Chang 2008). With more experience, faculty members tend to expand their use of other features, but the initial uses remain primary: the highest utilization is for providing course documents and one-way communication, much lower utilization is for discussion, and the lowest utilization is for interactivity or synchronous communication. Communication features are "poorly utilized in most institutions, the LMSs being used primarily as storage facilities for lecture notes and PowerPoint presentations" (Sclater 2008). Current usage does not seem to meet student demands as society moves into greater use of web technology as a communication tool, nor does it impact learning. In a nationwide survey of department chairs, over half indicated that although CMSs take much more time to use than traditional teaching without online support, there was no indication of increases in student learning; the systems were adopted for the convenience of the student rather than enhancing instruction (Harrington, Gordon, and Schibik 2004). It should be no surprise, then, that student satisfaction with the CMS has decreased over the last several years (Smith, Salaway, and Caruso 2009).

Faculty and administrators tend to focus on the features available in a CMS, but these studies indicate that how instructors approach the system may be more important than what features it offers. The key to accessing the potential of a CMS is to determine the pedagogy first, then look to the CMS to satisfy those goals. The reason CMSs are primarily used for administrative tasks is because instructors are forced to deal with the technology first. Educational CMSs were initially used by innovative educators, the "early adopters" of online teaching technologies who tended to bring their pedagogical problems to be solved through technology. According to Richard Katz: "The CMS has shifted from being based on the bottoms-up energy of a small cadre of inventive faculty to being the embodiment of a top-down institutional strategy" (2003, 9). Instructors coming to online teaching for the first time are often presented with the CMS itself, rather than information or philosophies for developing online pedagogies. Depending on their own experience with online technologies, the assumption is that they should take their traditional course and somehow plug it into the system. The focus is on uploading material rather than developing an approach.

It has become clear that CMSs must themselves be managed by instructors trying to advance their class goals. This is particularly true as the quantity and features of systems expand (Chapman 2005). Design limitations and usability challenges are always inherent in these systems (Kilker 2009). The instructor's pedagogical goals must always come first in developing any course, followed by the decision of which technologies to use. Nowhere is this more important than in the usage of a CMS. Instructors should focus first on their learning objectives, then engage the technology in a feedback loop without being intimidated by a monolithic system. All CMSs can become LMSs.

Which CMS?

The brands of CMS that faculty members are likely to encounter are limited. The market for integrated CMSs has been dominated until recently by vendors offering proprietary products. Proprietary CMSs have closed code, meaning that only the vendor may upgrade or change the product. In order to distinguish their product, vendors point to the number of installations and users and strive to make their CMS seem different from the others (Chapman 2005). A number of efforts have been made to provide meaningful comparisons among the various products; the most widely used is EduTools (www.edutools.info). CMS features change rapidly, and such comparisons may be meaningless unless an instructor is looking for a particular set of features. Most integrated systems include the following features:

- uploading of materials in various formats,
- a set navigation scheme that can be customized,
- delivery and statistical analysis of various types of assessments,
- delivery and management of asynchronous discussion,
- support for foreign languages, and
- management interfaces for grades and enrollment.

Blackboard and WebCT, now part of the same company, dominate market share for these systems; a majority of colleges use Blackboard as their primary CMS. The default setup for both systems focuses on the organization of course materials by type, such as Course Content, Communication, and Tools (Beatty and Ulasewicz 2006, 41). More features are added with each update: one recent addition to Blackboard is a closed social bookmarking feature called Scholar. Security is a primary asset of proprietary systems such as Blackboard/Web CT. They can be tied into the student information system at the institution, and students can use the same password for the CMS and other access points for the college. Other proprietary systems, such as Desire2Learn (a Canadian product), have become competitive enough to threaten Blackboard/WebCT, as evidenced by a 2006 lawsuit brought by Blackboard against Desire2Learn for infringement of its patent for an "Internet-Based Education Support

System and Methods" (U.S. Patent No. 6,988,138). In general, proprietary CMSs focus on management and tend to be favored by colleges that want a large, centralized, controlled environment for online course offerings and have the staff to handle the continual updates.

Unlike proprietary products, open source systems are based on code that is freely available and can be adapted by a large community of users. The largest of these is the Sakai Project, which is developing a list of features that rivals Blackboard but focuses more on interactivity. Moodle, an LMS based on social constructivism as a learning model, is currently the most popular open source system among educators. Open source code also exists for blogs, wikis, and more specific applications. Faculty and designers often seek such code because they have a particular pedagogical goal in mind. Once adapted, the free code is available to those who have a similar objective. In general, open source software evolves quickly to follow trends in technology and usage and thus tends to boast features supporting the most current uses of the web. In the case of Moodle, the more intuitive interface is the result of large groups of users contributing usability suggestions. However, open source systems tend to require a dedicated programmer to adapt them to the specific needs of the institution; they also demand considerable investment in time, money, and expertise. Even without going into the intricacies of code and system adaptation, it is still possible to put pedagogy first in a proprietary CMS. The key is to use the features effectively in support of pedagogical goals.

Adapting CMS Features

Syllabus and Navigation

Instructors invariably construct syllabus-type documents for their on-site classes, so many continue this approach online. Blackboard is often first used to post the course syllabus, either as a print-ready word-processed document or as a webpage. Traditionally, a syllabus contains not only a schedule and reading assignments, but also statements about class and institutional policies (attendance, grade distribution, disabled student services, etc.). On paper, it provides a handy packet of reference for the instructor and student. Online, such a syllabus creates several screens of text that must be scrolled, increasing the likelihood that students will not read all the material, and it contains many different types of information.

For ease of reading and reference, instructors could consider breaking up the syllabus into sections, each with its own navigation button, in order to make it more readable; creating the syllabus as a web page with links (an interactive syllabus) to accomplish the same goal but with a different look; or rethinking the whole idea of a syllabus entirely.

In Moodle, for example, the entire main page could be considered the syllabus. In "weekly" format, the dates are there, and everything can be organized like a calendar, with blocks of other information at the sides of the screen. In Blackboard or WebCT, it is possible to reduce the navigation buttons to just a few (or even just one) and have the default page be the syllabus, appearing as a page of links to all elements of the class.

Navigation, the way a user moves around a site or webpage, at first seems to be determined by the CMS. The buttons on the left menu in Blackboard or Web CT, or the boxes in Moodle, indicate the default navigation, but it need not be used if it does not fit the instructor's pedagogy. It is possible to instead use buttons showing the weeks or units instead. The challenge with customization is to correct (or prevent) the need for numerous clicks to get to the information. Too much "drilling down" is frustrating for students and makes it easy to get lost. Instructors should customize the CMS navigation to mirror the way they think about the structure of their class, rather than letting the default navigation force them to conform to an awkward pattern. Figure 4.1 provides an example, with Blackboard's default menu on the left and a customized menu on the right.

Presentation and Information: The "Content"

Although some technologists consider anything inside a CMS to be content, most educators use the term to refer only to presentation elements rather than interactive elements. Thus content would include text written by the instructor, images, and multimedia such as audio or video files, animations, and slideshows. Such elements might be created by the instructor, a publisher, or an outside source. They can be uploaded into the system or linked out by the system to wherever they are on the web. A number of instructors and educational experts have been disappointed that CMS platforms are most often used as simply a container for content; they seem to be "trapped content silos" rather than learning platforms (Lamberson and Lamb 2003).

There are ways to make presentation material more accessible and useful. Pedagogical units or topics should have all the appropriate infor-

Figure 4.1   **Default and Customized Blackboard Menus**

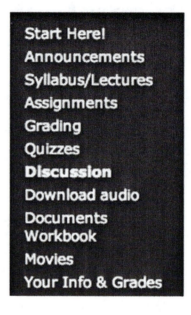

mational and interactive elements grouped together. In an on-site class, a lecture can be highly interactive, inviting student participation throughout before it is followed by assessment—why not use this approach online? For example, a unit on Topic 3 could contain the readings, online lecture, discussion forum, and quiz as a set. If such elements are divided and each put into its own default section of the CMS ("Course Documents," "Readings," "Quizzes"), both students and instructor tend to consider each presentation element as distinct from the interactive elements of the class, and even distinct from other elements in the same unit. Effective online pedagogy is based on "chunking" material—offering it in small bites— and the topic or unit is the construct many classroom faculty use. Most CMSs, however, organize material by type rather than unit. This may be why some scholars consider CMSs as a threat to pedagogical independence and faculty power (Katz 2003, 9). Instructors should be able to organize their course as they see fit. Moodle attempts to make this task easier with its boxlike structure, permitting the information and presentation pages, discussion forum, chat, branches lesson, and other elements to appear as a list of links in the box for that week or section. This approach can be

Figure 4.2   **Blackboard Mini html Editor**

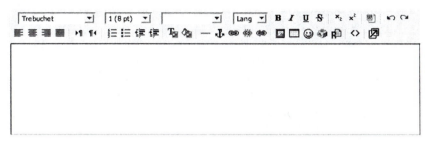

replicated in Blackboard by changing the buttons and creating pages with links—yet another reason to customize the course menu.

There is also the question of where the content is located. The default location for course files is usually the server associated with the CMS, but this is far from ideal for later retrieval. Most CMSs make it easy to create materials inside the program. When the instructor adds a page or item, a mini html editor is often available on the screen (see Figure 4.2).

Entering text directly into the CMS can create pages for the syllabus and other course content. When adding images, the user is usually prompted to upload the images into the system from the local hard drive. The difficulty with uploading content is that these text and images then reside in the system. Text entered directly into Blackboard, for example, would reside on the college's Blackboard server, as would any uploaded images. While this may be convenient, it can create a problem when changing systems or trying to move material from place to place. It is very rare that content can be moved easily from one system to another, especially among proprietary systems (Chapman 2005). The intent of the vendor is to keep users dependent on the product.

The simplest solution is to avoid creating a great deal of content inside the system. All text, image files, and multimedia should be developed and stored externally whenever possible. Doing this can be as simple as keeping a folder of all files on the instructor's local hard drive and using copy-and-paste to put items into the CMS form fields. Instructors with more computer experience may prefer to upload their files to a server separate from the LMS and link out to their content items. If space on the college server is limited or access is highly restricted due to security concerns, it may be desirable to purchase space on an externally hosted site (typical cost is about $10 a month). This can be especially useful for instructors who work at more than one college, who may find updating and moving materials on several college servers to be inconvenient, to say the least. Even if the college mandates the use of its own CMS, college-specific pages and sites can link out to these resources, and the instructor need update them in only one place. Caveats of this method would include, of course, lack of technical support for externally hosted files. There might also be concerns about intellectual property, unless it is certain that the instructors own their own content. Such concerns may become passé soon, since some experts think that the LMS of the future will have to allow for greater import and export of materials, to interface better with web applications, in order to survive commercially (Sclater 2008).

Interactivity and Assessment

CMSs all have ways of supporting communication between students and instructors, individually and collectively. Most have an email or messaging function for private correspondence between the teacher and the individual student. Instructor-to-group messages can take place through webpages or broadcast features such as Announcements (Blackboard) or Latest News (Moodle). To work most effectively, instructors should use the most appropriate tools for their communication style. Messaging keeps the individual private contact inside the course itself, which some may find convenient, while others prefer email.

Current research suggests encouraging social interaction among students is an effective way to promote learning. This may be done inside the CMS or apart from it. Online learning can be isolating, since each student works from a different location. All contact is computer-mediated, and it is difficult to access the physical cues that give deeper meaning to communication. Without carefully designed interaction, the online course becomes nothing more than an electronic version of a correspondence course by mail or a tutorial for training, rather than an opportunity to use what the online experience has to offer learners. Current research on learning styles indicates that young people in particular require social interaction in order to learn.

Which tool is best for social interaction? All CMSs have some type of asynchronous bulletin-board-style forum or discussion, and some have synchronous chat features. Some now have internal blogs or journals with commenting features. The pedagogy, again, should determine the choice of tool. Asynchronous discussions can take place over a period of time, and students can access them at any point. They allow for more reflection, but they have to be carefully guided so they do not become bulletin boards, with the initial postings answering the questions and the rest parroting. They can also be visually problematic, since the default is to allow the opening of only one message at a time, and determining who is replying to whom can be as difficult as recalling the thread of an extensive conversation. One study indicates that students lose context completely as they focus on reading only the most recent posts, an approach encouraged by the CMS tagging those messages as unread (Hewitt 2003, 32). Most CMSs have features allowing posts to be collected and viewed together, though these vary in quality and the ability to display the context properly (i.e., which posts are replying to which). There are often more options than are immediately apparent. For example, Moodle's "nesting" design lends itself well to discussion of a single topic because everyone can easily see the entire conversation on one screen.

Synchronous chat and the use of web-based conferencing tools such as Elluminate or Wimba require students to be online at a certain time and to have the technology operational at that time. Some systems exist inside the CMS, while others can be linked out. Chat is very much "on the fly" in format, and instructors should be comfortable with the sort of colloquial communication endemic to the chat medium, while at the same time learning to guide a freewheeling conversation into something more structured. Chat works best with a limited number of students, usually no more than eight. Its advantage is immediacy, the necessity of students to engage fully and quickly, and the chance for students to ask questions and explore ideas while communicating with others directly. It is most suitable for discussions that would take place within a limited period of time in the classroom, rather than something requiring more reflection.

Interaction with content could be as simple as a self-assessment following a lecture or as complex as a simulation or branched lesson that leads students through the material. According to Hamish Coates at the University of Michigan: "LMSs have the capacity to influence how students engage with their study and to change collaboration, communication, and access to learning materials" (2005, 66). Engagement with the material itself can be as important, or more important, than collaboration with colleagues or the passive exposure to presentation materials. The pathway through the content is an integral part of an instructor's pedagogy, and it should not be dictated by the technology. Blackboard's default is a linear path through content, but all LMSs can be adapted to create problem-based paths instead (Harrington, Gordon, and Schibik 2004, 311). Moodle's lessons provide a way to guide students through pages based on their responses to objective questions. A flash animation for a particular topic that allows students to explore and test their knowledge can be both engaging and enjoyable. Coates notes, however, that few institutions consider how students learn when evaluating or purchasing a CMS (2005, 68). This lack of focus is evident in the design for interactivity within these systems, which tends to be haphazard. There are few "wizards" or tutorials within CMSs that can assist the instructor with creating valuable interactions with content; thus doing so requires more planning and design from the instructor.

Assessment can assist in this regard. Moodle's branched lessons provide a good example: at each stage, points can be given and recorded in the Grades section. Tests can be learning opportunities as well as changed to earn points. Self-assessment and pretesting are valuable in offsetting student fears about testing in an online system. As a practical matter, just as with content, it is important for instructors to design both pretesting and actual exams outside the LMS. Specific formats can be used to ease the importing of questions for use in pools or collections. The need to design outside the system and import content is nowhere more important than with quizzes and tests—this is the area where each CMS traps instructors. Each can import a selection of formats, though the selection differs from system to system. Plain text is usually the best format for saving, then adapting to the system. Blackboard test generators, available on the websites of a few colleges for everyone to use, can translate text into format acceptable for loading into that system.

Less traditional assessments can be suitable in the online environment when they fit the instructor's pedagogy. Online portfolios are becoming more popular for tracking the work of students at a single institution; the approach is being used effectively in teacher education, where students create a portfolio to show future employers how standards were met. At a smaller level, online portfolios that feature student work throughout the semester can count for a portion of the grade or replace the final examination. Portfolios and self-assessments can be housed in student blogs (either public to course members or private) or posted in discussion. They can be individual or based on collaborative projects, which could be developed in a wiki or other collaborative document program that allows groups to edit a document. Again, few CMSs offer such social features, although they are beginning to appear. As the social construction of knowledge becomes more accepted as essential for lifelong learning, these systems may be forced to include such elements or find themselves abandoned for more interactive alternatives. Blackboard is now integrating read-write components such as wikis, blogs, and bookmark sharing into the CMS. But these tools are still used inside the "closed silo," where they cannot be viewed by outsiders nor accessed after the course is over. Instructors who see their course as a closed space, protected from outsiders, will enjoy using such built-in tools to foster greater learning. Those who want elements of their course (or the entire course) open to the larger web, who have pedagogies based on broader learning communities, may choose to link out instead to such collaborative tools. Again, the key is the instructor's set of teaching objectives.

"Accidental Pedagogy" and Inspiration

Despite their limitations, CMSs can also provide inspiration. Access to features never before used by the instructor can cause a rethinking of approaches and assignments. Instructors willing to explore the software can discover tools such as voice chat, branched lessons, and social bookmarking that they might consider using to achieve a particular goal. Exposure to tools, while it should not determine the pedagogy, can create innovation through the intellectual stimulation they engender. "Accidental pedagogy," a concept coined by Glenda Morgan (2003), is the idea that continuing use of a CMS can lead to discovery and changes in the pedagogy. This is why "playing," or experimenting with the web and with CMSs, is important not only to technological proficiency but also to creativity. Maintaining as much independence as possible from any particular CMS, having exposure to a number of different systems, and exploring alternatives makes teaching more flexible and more open to inspiration from a wide variety of sources.

Thus instructors should never limit their knowledge to a single CMS or even to such systems in general. Because it is a great deal of work to create courses in a variety of systems, instructors might consider gaining experience through their own web-based professional development. More and more teachers are using the interactivity and convenience of the "read-write web" to construct their own personal learning environments. Personal start pages (such as Pageflakes or Netvibes) can help instructors gather the information they need, such as RSS (Really Simple

Syndication) feeds from journals and collections of bookmarks. Online or desktop RSS feed aggregators (Google Reader, Feedraider) and social bookmarking services (such as del.icio.us or Diigo) can help organize vast resources. Free blog services (Edublogs, Blogger) can provide instructors an opportunity to express their ideas publicly and get feedback from others. All of these items can help instructors develop their own web experience so as to inform their effective use of CMSs.

Training Versus Adaptation

CMSs can be managed and made to work for most teaching methods. While various systems for delivering online classes have existed for at least twenty years, the merging of the two largest systems, Blackboard and WebCT, effectively limited commercial competition. Most colleges support one of these systems and provide training in how to use it. However, there is a difference between training in how to use a piece of technology and understanding how to translate pedagogy into a CMS. Technology trainers tend to be experts in helping people learn how to use tools, not how to apply pedagogical practices or teach a particular discipline. Talking to experienced online faculty, attending workshops (many are offered online by groups dedicated to online teaching, such as the Teaching, Learning, and Technology Group at www.tltgroup.org), and reading articles about effective practices are as important as learning how to use the system.

At the same time, an instructor's pedagogy may make it advisable to heavily adapt or avoid such systems. A number of colleges offer only one CMS to their faculty and support only that system. Thus many faculty members assume that they must use that CMS, which may not be the case in terms of actual policy. Web-based applications or an externally hosted server can be an excellent option, especially for part-time faculty who work at different colleges. Hosting companies sometimes offer open source CMS packages. A college's standard CMS can be used by the savvy faculty member as nothing more than a portal that refers the student to the instructor's CMS or website, which can be hosted elsewhere. If instructors abandon the CMS entirely, there is always the risk that students might complain about using technologies that differ from those in other classes. However, students' desire for "convenience" is similar to instructors' use of only the administrative elements in a CMS (Weaver, Spratt, and Nair 2008)—it does not necessarily improve learning. On the contrary, the technology skill set that will be expected of today's students in their future careers will require the ability to adapt basic skills to different systems, and almost all web applications are based on the same web skills as every CMS: clicking on links, clicking to open a panel to insert something, and so on. A more significant concern, however, is the lack of technical support. When choosing an external blog or wiki, for example, the instructor becomes the support person by default. In a hybrid class, this may not be a problem, since difficulties can often be worked out during the on-site portion of the course. Online, students will email the instructor when they encounter problems. The instructor can offer solutions by providing a place for students to discuss any problems and help each other and by becoming very familiar with the technology being implemented for student use.

At colleges where the proffered CMS must be used, working with and adapting the program extensively becomes crucial. Faculty should make themselves aware of the many new features being added to these programs, including social networking modules such as blogs and social bookmarking. In addition, since the major CMS interfaces have course menu buttons that can be linked to external URLs, an external collaborative site (such as Flickr or Ning) can be made to appear as if it were inside the CMS window. Thus it is possible to provide students with consistent navigation while still creating opportunities for learning that are not provided by the CMS itself. As instructors themselves become more familiar with the web tools offered for online learning, they will integrate them into their LMS or use them exclusively as learning environments, creating a greater variety of opportunities for student success.

Note

1. For discussion of ways in which the CMS can determine pedagogy for novice instructors, see Lane (2008, 2009). http://firstmonday.org/htbin/cgiwrap/bin/ojs/index.php/fm/article/view/2530/2303.

References

Beatty, Brian, and Connie Ulasewicz. 2006. "Online Teaching and Learning in Transition: Faculty Perspectives on Moving From Blackboard to the Moodle Learning Management System." *TechTrends* 50, no. 4: 36–45.

Chapman, Diane. 2005. "Introduction to Learning Management Systems." In *Encyclopedia of Distance Learning* 3: 1149–1155. Hershey, PA: Idea Group Reference.

Chang, Chinhong Lim. 2008. "Faculty Perceptions and Utilization of a Learning Management System in Higher Education." PhD diss., College of Education, Ohio University.

Coates, Hamish. 2005. "Leveraging LMSs to Enhance Campus-Based Student Engagement." *EDUCAUSE Quarterly* 1: 66–68.

Downes, Stephen. 2005. "E-learning 2.0." *eLearn Magazine*. www.elearnmag.org/subpage.cfm?article=29-1&section=articles.

Feldstein, Michael. 2006. "Unbolting the Chairs: Making Learning Management Systems More Flexible." *eLearn Magazine*. www.elearnmag.org/subpage.cfm?section=tutorials&article=22-1.

Gastfriend, Hilliard. 2005. "Faculty Use of Course Management Systems Survey: System Aggregate Report." University System of Georgia, November 15. www.alt.usg.edu/research/studies/cms.phtml.

Harrington, Charles F., Scott A. Gordon, and Timothy J. Schibik. 2004. "Course Management System Utilization and Implications for Practice: A National Survey of Department Chairpersons." *Online Journal of Distance Learning Administration* 7, no. 4. www.westga.edu/~distance/ojdla/winter74/harrington74.htm.

Hewitt, Jim. 2003. "How Habitual Online Practices Affect the Development of Asynchronous Discussion Threads."*Journal of Educational Computing Research* 28, no. 1: 31–45.

Katz, Richard N. 2003. "Balancing Technology and Tradition: The Example of Course Management Systems." *EDUCAUSE Review* 38, no. 4: 48–54, 56, 57–59.

Kilker, Julian. 2009. "Procrustean Pedagogy: The Architecture of Efficiency in a New Medium." In *Cultures of Efficiency,* ed. Sharon Kleinman, 212–229. New York: Peter Lang.

Lamberson, Michelle, and Brian Lamb. 2003. "Course Management Systems: Trapped Content Silos or Sharing Platforms?" In *Learning Objects: Contexts and Connections*, ed. Catherine M. Gynn and Stephen R. Acker, 59–75. Columbus: Ohio State University.

Lane, Lisa M. 2008. "Toolbox or Trap? Couse Management Systems and Pedagogy." *EDUCAUSE Quarterly* 31, no. 2: 4–6.

———. 2009. "Insidious Pedagory: How Course Management Systems Affect Treaching." *First Monday* 14, no. 10, October.

Morgan, Glenda. 2003. "Faculty Use of Course Management Systems." EDUCAUSE Center for Applied Research.

Sclater, Niall. 2008. "Web 2.0, Personal Learning Environments, and the Future of Learning Mangement Systems." EDUCAUSE Center for Applied Research, Research Bulletin, June 24. www.educause.edu/ir/library/pdf/ERB0813.pdf.

Siemens, George. 2004. "Connectivism: A Learning Theory for the Digital Age." December 12. www.elearnspace.org/Articles/connectivism.htm.

Smith, Shannon D., Gail Salaway, and Judith Borreson Caruso. 2009. "ECAR Study of Undergraduate Students and Information Technology, 2009." EDUCAUSE Center for Applied Research, Research Study, Vol. 6. www.educause.edu/Resources/TheECARStudyofUndergraduateStu/187215.

Weaver, Debbi, Christine Spratt, and Chenicheri Sid Nair. 2008. "Academic and Student Use of a Learning Management System: Implications for Quality." *Australasian Journal of Educational Technology* 24, no. 1: 30–41.

5

Blended Classrooms

Hybridity, Social Capital, and Online Learning

Peter Sands

For about twenty-five years the digital revolution in higher education has produced a steady stream of predictions: that handwriting
will disappear, that printed textbooks will transition to computerized
versions, that hypertext will become Vannevar Bush's (1945) memex
of interlinked information, that bricks-and-mortar institutions will be
shuttered because of a stampede to online-only education. Plato thought
writing would be the death of memory; nineteenth-century educators
thought replacing the slate would be the death of fundamental teaching
skills; today's prognosticators ought to have learned from the past. The
much-heralded wholesale change in higher education has turned out to
be accretive, additive, expansive, rather than supplanting "traditional"
modes of education.

Thus, American University in Washington, DC, reported in 2007 that
nearly all its online students were enrolled at the university for face-to-
face classes as well—attending American but also taking online courses
(Powers 2007). In my own online courses, I have rarely had any students
participating at a "distance" of more than a few miles. Nationally, the higher
education consulting firm Eduventures says that "more than one-third [of
online students] live within a 50-mile radius of their online education provider" and that two-thirds of online students are in the geographic region
of the university they attend online. Additionally, Eduventures reports that
"63% preferred an online provider to have some physical presence at least
within their state" (Eduventures 2007; Simonson 1996).

Why would this be so? Social capital.

Both critics and champions of the traditional university note that its
structural components and organization have remained largely unchanged

over most of the past millennium, at least when compared to other institutions.[1] Indeed, the physical site of the university remains the center of the higher education world. Whatever its disadvantages, this is largely a social and intellectual good that contributes to political, economic, and other goods in society. Further, the hybrid or blended model of online education is the best means of preserving the important social capital of higher education located in symbolically important institutional, physical spaces.

Hybrid courses are an innovative way to deliver essential content, but also to emphasize frequent writing by students in service of analyzing texts and images and making their own arguments in writing. Blended courses multiply the opportunities for feedback in different media and forums. They create additional opportunities for verbal and written interaction between and among students and teachers. These are among the most essential pedagogical tools of a liberal education: reading, writing, and arguing. The model has costs and benefits, requiring some infrastructure investment that is passed on to individual students, but also preserving the university's physical and social relationship with its community.

Online and Hybrid Courses

Purely online courses confer distinct advantages and disadvantages. While they enable students to time-shift and accommodate their education to the realities of their lives outside the classroom, they also shift much of the burden for time-management and direction of learning onto the student. They allow some students to gain access to otherwise inaccessible courses, but they also lead to a fairly high rate of attrition among students not self-directed enough to complete an online course.[2]

Blended, or hybrid, courses mix elements of online learning with face-to-face meetings, bringing otherwise disparate learners into contact with one another for common discussion of readings and other coursework. These courses still distribute much of the work of learning onto students—forcing, for example, visible and sustained engagement with the semester's reading by requiring weekly written assignments placed on a course wiki or posted to discussion boards on course management systems such as Desire2Learn (D2L) or Blackboard. These courses also enable students to do some time shifting in choosing when each week or even month to do the reading and written assignments. But they also continue to use the social capital of the university by bringing students and teachers together in the physical world of an actual university for discussion, question-and-answer, and other group activities. Thus they gain the advantages of both online courses and more traditional modes.

Online Courses: Advantages and Disadvantages

Both traditional and nontraditional students today have busier lives than students of the 1960s to the 1980s. Personal computers, cellular telephones, media players, and wireless networks have created nearly ubiquitous computing in developed nations. At the turn of the millennium, the global information and communication technologies (ICT) market was on track to exceed $3 trillion in the next half decade, a prediction that proved true even with the 2001 downturn in the dot-com economy (WITSA 2000, 2008). A stumbling economy has reduced the ability to pay while higher education costs have risen (National Center for Public Policy and Higher Education 2006). Americans live with reduced leisure time and reduced social safety nets, increasing both the amount of time they spend at work and the amount of their income that must go toward providing for needs such as health care that are provided for differently in other Western countries. People strapped for time are particularly likely to be drawn to online courses.[3]

Courses that do not require attendance at a given time and in a given place confer advantages on students. They do not have to drive or otherwise transport themselves to the university. They save on parking. They do not need a room on or near the campus. They do not have to arrange their daily schedules to meet the demands of the university. Cost savings for students are elusive, however. To attend courses online, students need to have access to a personal computer, a persistent Internet connection with sufficient bandwidth, and a personal life flexible enough to tolerate blurring lines between school and home—somewhat analogous to the blurring of home and work experienced by telecommuters. These are not insignificant costs, and the Eduventure report cited above suggests that students are bearing them as additional costs rather than savings.

However some advantages do accrue because of the very nature of online work. Online courses are largely conducted by reading and writing. Students in Richard Light's well-known study reported that the courses in which they wrote the most were the courses in which they learned the most—and which made the greatest subjective impressions of quality on them (Light 2001). But there is precious little writing in most face-to-face classes, in spite of the writing across the curriculum and writing in the disciplines movements. In well-designed online courses, however, successful students must engage with substantial amounts of text, both as readers and writers. They read, summarize, synthesize, write about, and apply disciplinary information. Such a course provides opportunities to read sustained arguments and discuss them in writing between and among students and teachers.

A Simple Sample Hybrid Course

Blended courses *are* more than simply extensions of the traditional model in which students have meetings as well as individual homework—reading the texts, writing essays, and completing problem sets. Instead, some of those individualized tasks are conducted in an open, Internet forum. At a minimum, this has an additive rather than supplanting effect by adding a component of public writing.

For example, students in a class that meets twice a week read assigned texts outside the classroom, then attend class for lectures, discussion, or other activities. They may or may not take notes on the material. Instructors may or may not assign written work or problem sets that address the material, and there will be varying levels of consequences and rewards for noncompletion or completion of those assignments. But in a hybrid setting, all these issues are openly exposed, creating a strong performance incentive for both teachers and students.

The hybrid setting distributes some of the time that is ordinarily occupied by classroom meetings into the rest of the week. Students in an active, writing-intensive hybrid course will not simply read more, or read more slowly to occupy that time. They will engage with the reading by completing assigned tasks—summaries, syntheses, analyses—and by putting their written work online for other students in the course to read and respond to. At designated times, that work will also be the focal point for in-class activities conducted by the teacher. This structure is worth elaborating a little further.

My hybrid courses typically meet once a week for the amount of time that is allotted for a twice-weekly course. If it is a film course, we have slightly longer meeting times to accommodate screenings. If it is a literature course or a writing workshop, we stick with the times dictated by my institution's scheduling. Students receive an explanation in their syllabus of what we will do with the additional time, as well as a written rationale for the structure I have built. Part of that rationale explains the time breakdown of two to four hours of preparation for every one hour of in-class time. I give them a chart and timeline that explains how the ordinary classroom hour has been distributed across the week and how weeks are distributed across a month. Each four-week period culminates in a written self-assessment in the form of a letter and response exchange with a small group of peers.

During the week, students have reading assignments and responsibility for either generating online discussion with a written response to the reading or keeping that discussion going with a written commentary on another student's response. These responses and commentaries are completed according to parameters and instructions they have received in writing, and are graded as simply acceptable or not acceptable. I can scan them at a glance to see if the student has completed the reading, has understood it, and is contributing to the ongoing written discussion. This portion of the class, which contributes one-half or one-third of their grade, is evaluated by the percentage of acceptable responses the student submits before the deadline each week.

This method ensures student participation. Only students who have done the reading—on time—can post an acceptable contribution. Students get a quick check on their work in two ways: they see that their submission has been read and marked acceptable by the instructor (or they receive email notification and explanation when it is not acceptable); they also can see whether their contribution attracts the attention of other students, who choose which posts to respond to. If teaching rhetorical strategies for dialogue in writing is best done in writing, simple Internet discussion boards and dialogue-intensive assignments hold significant promise.

Finally, the in-class meeting each week addresses key postings that students have made, integrating those comments with the lecture. I simply display selections from the online discussions at appropriate points in the lecture, projecting the text on a screen. The student authors read the selections aloud and then glosses them—repeating and expanding what they have posted online. Since students have written the texts themselves, they are prepared to repeat, explain, and defend their ideas. Most expand verbally on what they have said in writing, engaging in verbal give-and-take with peers who responded to them online—or who missed the original posting—during the classroom discussion. Such activities are a low-stakes means of creating, rewarding, and using student participation in service of learning.

So far, that sounds like an idealized version of the classroom, with students diligently working on their own and then coming together for a spirited discussion. Indeed, it is an idealized version. There are times when students whose postings are highlighted in class do not show up that day. There are students who cannot or will not elaborate on what they have written. There are students whose shyness in person prevents them from being as articulate as they are when they write online. Also there are students who react to the forced verbal participation with open hostility. Naturally, there are students who display versions of those negative behaviors online as well.

But it is more than an idealized version. There are real incentives and consequences for participation or failure to participate. Students report in their evaluations and self-assessments greater engagement because of the structured, disciplined, and participatory assignments. So why not just use a version of such assignments in a traditional classroom in place of homework? The simple answer: time.

The hybrid classroom acknowledges that there are inefficiencies in classroom information delivery models. Those models work on the assumption that telling is generally equivalent to teaching. This is not to say that an effective lecturer is an oxymoron. Rather than relying exclusively on monodirectional lecturing or even relatively structured Socratic questioning, the hybrid course situates lecturing in the context of very active student engagement with learning. Rather than relying on the teacher's ability to convey her considerable understanding and ability to apply knowledge, the hybrid course blends practice activities with the contextualizing, synthesizing, and applying that an effective lecture displays. Students themselves perform tasks substantially similar to those of the instructor. Students write summaries and engage each other in dialogue, displaying both comprehension and error. An effective lecturer in the hybrid classroom tailors the week's meeting to emphasize the material students have understood—reinforcement—while at the same time addressing clear problems: factual errors, misapplications, or gaps in needed historical or other contextual knowledge.

Physical Presence

Universities are designed spaces that encourage reverence and awareness of the power of the institution. They remind the individual that the enterprise is larger than the person, that there is historical continuity, economic power, and the brilliance of shared human enterprise in the building. They materialize abstractions: learning, governance, art, politics, and science.

In postmodern or posthumanist worldviews there is little reverence for such institutional trappings or for the grand narratives they replicate. Exclusivity, classism, gender bias, corporate cooptation, cozy government relationships, misuses of history and science in nationalist pursuits rightly appear in critiques of higher education. But there is also much to admire and retain about the long history of organized higher education. To condemn a human enterprise because of a historical error—or even a current error—is simplistic Manichaeanism. Ignoring the contributions of an institution and its members while emphasizing the negatives that accompany any complex enterprise over long periods of time raises only the specter of critical stasis rather than dynamic interaction between history, present, and future.

I do not intend to sentimentalize in making the point that such institutions have positive associations and effects. But statistical parsing or ethnographic observation cannot erase the simple fact that universities do inspire sentiments worth acknowledging and even exploiting. Both reverence and resentment toward the university generate consequent positive behaviors and effects. People travel and sacrifice time, money, and obligations to learn at a particular place; and not just Harvard or Cambridge or Oxford or Yale, but also at community colleges, liberal arts schools, and large land-grant research universities across the vast middle of the United States. Higher education has social value because it has demonstrable effects in real dollars over a person's lifetime earnings. But it also has intangible values stemming from exposure of individuals to unfamiliar ideas, to the tapestry of history, to mathematics and sciences. Those intangible values at the heart of a liberal education situate people in their culture and relation to other cultures.

Mixing Worlds

While purely online courses confer scheduling advantages on students and distribute time-management problems more equally among teachers and students, they also run the risk of isolating learners and of propagating misunderstandings. A simple thought experiment shows one possible problem. In a group of twenty people, one person asks a question that reveals a fundamental misunderstanding. Let us say that the misunderstanding is largely unavoidable because of inadequate contextual information—such as an assumption by the professor based on a generational cultural awareness not shared by his students—and is also largely hidden. Or say that the misunderstanding comes from students taking courses out of sequence in an ostensibly sequenced curriculum.

If the misunderstanding is revealed in a group setting, the professor can efficiently correct it for the whole group in a number of ways: explanation or lecture, group activity or problem-solving, assignment of additional reading and a follow-up discussion. But if the misunderstanding is revealed in a one-on-one, online discussion, even when that discussion takes place in a distributed, open environment such as a bulletin board to which all students post, the efficiencies are much curtailed. There is no guarantee that all students will pay attention—that they will read the discussion post in question, that they will understand the issue, that they will correct their misunderstanding. There is no guarantee that a busy professor will necessarily catch the error when it first appears. The messy nature of human cognition and learning communicated in language guarantees such problems. In the online classroom, teachers can largely replicate efficient lecturing or whole-group conversations and activities. But because of the inefficiencies—or higher signal-to-noise ratio—of distributed learning, there is more fail-safe built into classrooms that combine online and face-to-face settings to take advantage of the strengths of both. The missing element in the purely online classroom is oral dialogue—involving both sight and sound—and physical colocation in space and time. There is something useful still about a bunch of people going to a single place in the universe, together, with a purpose. When students read and write, they may benefit from being with others, but also they certainly might benefit from doing those tasks in the quiet of homes and libraries, at times they can schedule on their own, and at paces that suit individuals. But when students encountering material for the first time have collective questions or have collective needs for information transmission or can achieve understanding through collective action—such as completing problems or participating in free-flowing discussions—those objectives are best achieved by a balancing act: between online or individual time and face-to-face time.

We gather together for many reasons, some historical and habitual, some cultural, and some practical. There is a long tradition of meeting at a designated time and place to teach and learn. In ancient times this was a necessity. In modern times it is, depending on your point of view, a luxury or a continuing necessity or part of a set of useful practices. Culturally, we have invested enormous powers in formal gatherings and gathering places—churches, stadiums, government buildings, libraries, and universities. To emphasize the solemnity and importance of the task, to convey the power of knowledge, to acknowledge the long historical connections among churches, governments, and schools, we make use of the physical spaces of the university to gather people with the appropriate credentials and seriousness to pursue higher education. Practically speaking, it is easier to manage learning as a shared enterprise deeply implicated in other practices—including economic—in the culture if that learning takes place largely at designated times and in designated spaces. The eighteenth-century rise of disciplinary society—whether the Foucauldian narrative of power and struggle or a more mundane observation of the development of grid-based scheduling and planning technologies—remains with us today because it is, simply, an efficient way of managing people and time.

There is, too, a presumption that gathering together under the auspices of a learning institution and its authority figures—the faculty—answers a human need for purposeful connection with other human beings. Whether such needs are adequately met by other social activities is an open question. Americans increasingly do not participate in the social interactions of past generations, to the detriment of society as a whole (Putnam 2001). Without shared activities, civil society reaches neither consensus nor dissensus; it fractures.

People should have a healthy skepticism toward institutions, authority figures, and master narratives. Higher education faculty members need skepticism toward our corporatized public institutions increasingly bereft of public funding. But the wholesale termination of such institutions would be shortsighted at best and hypocritical at worst. We do not need to do away with such institutions and hierarchies, at least not entirely. We need places of reverence, places where there is a significant investment of social and cultural capital sufficient to create and sustain civic relationships. We need places where people are expected to think, innovate, study, explain, and question. We need places where others go to learn to think, innovate, study, explain, and question. And we need those places to be visible reminders of a world that encompasses both the practicality of patentable, licensable, useful technologies and the abstractions of ethics, aesthetics, histories, and ideas.

Notes

1. New York University president John Sexton, interviewed by Stephen Colbert, quipped that "of the 85 institutions in the world that exist today the way they did 500 years ago, 70 of them are universities" (2006).

2. A figure of 10 to 20 percent higher attrition rates for online courses is frequently seen in the literature. See, for example, Angelino and Williams (2007). In support of their figures, Angelino and Williams cite Carr (2000) and Moody (2004).

3. The literature is fairly clear on this, but anecdotal reports such as the series that National Public Radio ran in the fall of 2007 also bring the point home (Abramson 2007). A decade ago, empirical research already suggested that distance students tended to be older and driven by different concerns than traditional college-age students (Thompson 1998). Currently, such assertions have the character of received wisdom (Skopek and Schuhmann 2008).

References

Abramson, Larry. 2007. "Online Courses Catch On in U.S. Colleges." NPR November 28, 2007. www.npr.org/templates/story/story.php?storyId=16638700).

Angelino, Lorraine M., and Frankie Keels Williams. 2007. "Strategies to Engage Online Students and Reduce Attrition Rates." *Journal of Educators Online* 4, no. 2. www.thejeo.com/Archives/Volume4Number2/Angelino%20Final.pdf.

Bush, Vannevar. 1945. "As We May Think." *Atlantic Online*, July 1945, www.theatlantic.com/unbound/flashbks/computer/bushf.htm.

Carr, Sarah. 2000. "As Distance Education Comes of Age, the Challenge Is Keeping the Students." *Chronicle of Higher Education*, February 11.

Eduventures Inc. 2007. "Geography Matters in Online Higher Education." http://eduventures.com/about/press/news-1/news_03_28_07.

Light, Richard J. 2001. *Making the Most of College: Students Speak Their Minds.* Cambridge, MA: Harvard University Press.

Moody, Johnette. 2004. "Distance Education: Why Are the Attrition Rates So High?" *Quarterly Review of Distance Education* 5, no. 3: 205–210.

National Center for Public Policy and Higher Education. 2006. "Measuring Up 2006: The National Report Card on Higher Education." http://measuringup.highereducation.org/nationalpicture/.

Powers, Elia. 2007. "News: Latest Twist in Distance Ed—Inside Higher Ed." *Inside Higher Education.* http://insidehighered.com/news/2007/08/09/american.

Putnam, Robert D. 2001. *Bowling Alone: The Collapse and Revival of American Community.* New York: Simon & Schuster.

Sexton, John. 2006. Interview by Stephen Colbert. *Colbert Report*, December 6.

Simonson, Michael. 1996. "Distance Education: Trends and Redefinition." *Frontiers in Education: Conference 1996 Proceedings* 2: 549–552.

Skopek, Tracy A., and Robert A. Schuhmann. 2008. "Traditional and Non-Traditional Students in the Same Classroom? Additional Challenges of the Distance Education Environment." *Online Journal of Distance Learning Administration* 11, no. 1. www.westga.edu/~distance/ojdla/spring111/skopek111.html.

Thompson, Melody M. 1998. "Distance Learners in Higher Education." In *Distance Learners in Higher Education: Institutional Responses for Quality Outcomes*, ed. Chere Campbell Gibson, 10–18. Madison, WI: Atwood.

WITSA. 2000. *Digital Planet 2000: The Global Information Economy.* November. www.witsa.org/DP2000sum.pdf.

———. 2008. *Digital Planet 2008.* May. www.witsa.org/v2/media_center/pdf/DigitalPlanet2008_ExecutiveSummary.pdf.

6

Facilitating Interaction in the Online Environment

Michelle Kilburn

As I began working on my first online course in the spring of 2005, I remember looking at the blinking cursor on my screen and thinking: "How are my students going to know I'm really here and not just 'turning on' my course and letting it run itself while I sit on the beach somewhere? By the end of the semester, are they going to feel like they know my computer better than they know me? Am I really going to get to know my students by chatting and typing through email?" All kinds of questions and issues began pouring over me, and as a result I spent quite a bit of time searching in the literature and talking to other online instructors for answers. This chapter is a conglomeration of literature review, personal experiences, and best practices that I have accrued as an online instructor, a certified online course evaluator, interim instructional designer, and former director of Southeast Online at Southeast Missouri State University. My goal is not only to review the research indicating the attributes of a good online course, but also to offer a few suggestions to aid instructors in creating a course in which students feel connected not only to each other, but also to the material, the instructor, and the technology.

The question of how to interact with students is a challenge for many new online instructors. For me, the challenge was to get "myself" into the class—beyond simply sending my students the textbook, list of assignments, and exams. I needed to find a way to create an active presence that would leave no doubt that I was present and participating in my online course. The guidelines I chose to follow were Moore and Kearsley's (2004) three primary types of interaction in distance education: student-to-content, student-to-instructor, and student-to-student. Hillman, Willis, and Gunawardena (1994) add a fourth type of interaction, student-to-interface, specifically delineated for web-based courses. In the upcoming section of this chapter, each type of interaction will be discussed, along with its impact on designing and developing an online course. The four types are certainly not mutually exclusive, particularly in the online environment, but I feel they help categorize and organize pedagogical goals.

Student-to-Content

Student-to-content interaction occurs as students examine and study the course materials (Moore and Kearsley 2004). As students move from the traditional classroom experience to an online learning format, they are faced with making the transition from a relatively passive learning experience to a more active one. For example, instead of listening to lectures, taking notes, and making presentations, online students must become adept at comprehending text-based material, obtaining material from multiple sources (Internet research, outside readings, etc.), and effectively utilizing discussion boards. The online instructor cannot simply glance out into the crowd and search for confused faces to obtain feedback on how students comprehend the material. Likewise, students cannot simply raise their hand during a lecture and ask for clarification. For an online instructor, serving as a facilitator to guide students through the material and providing feedback regarding their progress appear to be key elements in maintaining student interaction with the course content (Conrad 2002; Gulbahar and Yildirim 2006; Leasure, Davis, and Thievon 2000; Moore and Kearsley 2004; Sanders and Morrison-Shetlar 2001; Swan 2001).

In putting together online course materials, the first thing that may come to mind is assigning readings in the textbook, often followed by inclusion of outside resources. One important thing to remember is that students have enrolled in *your* course. They will benefit from your knowledge and expertise as much as, or even more than, they will from the textbook. Instructors must consider how they will infuse themselves into the course materials throughout the semester—for example, by incorporating those stories and theoretical explanations that they have relied on in face-to-face courses. Such material will not only help students interact with the content of the course, but also help them comprehend the materials—not to mention, let them know that the instructor's knowledge and expertise is present in the course.

Conrad (2002) found that online learners want a lot of course information up front, preferably before the course even begins. A new online instructor might overlook the importance of the first day of class introductions, the review of the course syllabus, class rules, and so on, or even the "housekeeping" discussions that typically take place during the first five minutes of every class period. However, these are critical pieces of information that online students need in order to be successful in their potentially new environment. I have found it useful to direct all students to a "Start Here" or "Getting Started" page that walks them step-by-step through the course and materials. One essential topic is how to access the course materials and resource links, such as the university's library, writing center, learning enrichment center, and electronic files. I also include the course syllabus and assignment information. The goal is to give students everything they need to get started and a roadmap on how to work their way through the course. Swan (2001) suggests that a key to enhancing learner-content interactions appears to be clarity of course design. Streamlining the course content and making it as simple to follow as possible may enhance the student-to-content interactions and help compensate for the lack of face-to-face meetings.

Another way to encourage student interaction with the content is to offer multiple self-assessment opportunities (i.e., short quizzes, exercises, activities). In my courses, I have at least one quiz for every chapter. The quizzes are not terribly intensive; the purpose is just to give students feedback on how they comprehend the material. It is more of a self-test for them than an evaluation tool for me. I also allow them to take each quiz up to three times and I record their highest score. The rationale behind the multiple opportunities to take the quiz is that the students are working with course materials and reviewing course content up to three times. Sanders and Morrison-Shetlar (2001) discovered that a majority of students prefer online quizzes as opposed to paper quizzes. I have found that students like the opportunity to retake the quizzes and appreciate being able to review the materials again.

While on the subject of assessment, I feel it is important to note that an online exam will often be different from face-to-face exams. Unless a proctor is required, students will have access to all course materials. Key word recognition and memorization questions may thus not meet the same objective in an online course as they do in a face-to-face course. Questions that require students to process and apply their new knowledge often prove the most beneficial.

Students often like a wide variety of material placed online for their use (Gulbahar and Yildirim 2006). Online instructors have a wealth of resources that have never been at their disposal in a face-to-face course. It bears noting that Chen, Wong, and Hsu (2003) caution that too much information available online can hinder student learning. Just because the information is out there, available with just a few clicks of the mouse, does not mean that students need to access it all. Information overload can be just as detrimental to the learning process as not providing enough information. If I am providing a link that I feel students might find interesting but that is not going to be on an exam or part of the evaluation process, I indicate it as such. Otherwise, students might click random link after link and end up getting tangled up in the World Wide Web. I try to keep in mind that students are looking to me to provide the roadmap that will allow them to navigate through the course.

There are multiple ways to provide content in an online course. Utilizing a variety of strategies can address multiple learning styles. A mixture of text-based, video-based, and activity-based materials not only breaks up the monotony for students, but also gives multiple formats that can be conducive to knowledge transfer. For example, using screen-capturing programs, a lecture can be recorded with PowerPoint, audio, or video; or complicated problems can be worked out and discussed by an instructor. PowerPoint outlines and other "handouts" can be made available so students can take notes as they review the material.

Providing a checklist of sorts that details dates, readings, assignments, and objectives enables students to navigate through the course and be assured that they have completed all the activities, have mastered each topic, and are ready to move on to the next topic or section. This kind of guidance is particularly useful for new online students who might feel anxious about their new learning environment.

Interaction with the course content is the foundation to establishing a good learning environment for online students. However, the elements that distinguish online classes from traditional correspondence courses are the opportunities for student-to-instructor and student-to-student interactions. According to Fredericksen et al. (2000), there is a positive relationship between the amount of interaction with the instructor and the student's perceived level of learning.

Student-to-Instructor

While we have established the importance of student-to-content interaction, students may not necessarily feel connected to the class from just sitting down and reading material on a computer screen or submitting assignments to an impersonal dropbox. Online instructors may feel that they are interacting with their students through lectures and assignments, but Dennen, Darabi, and Smith (2007) found that successful student-to-instructor interaction includes three elements: (1) maintaining frequency of contact, (2) having a regular presence in online class discussion, and (3) providing clear expectations to learners. Let us examine each of these elements individually.

Maintaining Frequency of Contact

An instructor's responsiveness (answering emails and providing feed-back) and message tone or style can affect a student's perception of instructor presence (Russo and Campbell 2004). Students who receive prompt feedback from their instructor report positive perceptions of learner-instructor interactions (Thurmond et al. 2002). Once they have participated or submitted their assignments, students like to receive both qualitative and quantitative feedback about their performance (Dennen 2005). The more details and feedback that can be provided for students, the more opportunities they have to experience interaction with the instructor. By simply opening the gradebook and accessing their grade for an assignment, students may not necessarily feel a connection with their instructor. Reading through detailed explanations on how they obtained that grade, however, will provide a much more personal interaction opportunity between the instructor and the students.

It has also been reported that students like seeing a photo and hearing an instructor's voice. Students indicate that it gives them a feeling of greater connection to the instructor's real-world presence (Russo and Campbell 2004). Using a screen and video capturing program, I post a short weekly video announcement to students as a way to: (1) let students see me and recognize that I am a real person; (2) conduct housekeeping activities, such as reminders of upcoming assignment and due dates; (3) provide "just-in-time" comments and discussion about topics that need further explanation or clarification; and (4) discuss current events that are relevant to the course. These weekly video announcements reinforce the point that I am here, active, and enthusiastic about the course. Concannon, Flynn, and Campbell (2005) found that instructors' enthusiasm for online learning has a motivating effect on their students.

Having a Regular Presence in Online Class Discussion

As in a face-to-face class, not all online communications focus on the content or the pedagogy of the course. Other instructor roles are managerial, social, and technical (Berge 1995; Bonk et al. 2001; Darabi, Sikorski, and Harvey 2006). Although it is obvious that these roles might not directly be linked to learning, they are necessary to reduce or eliminate learning barriers. Especially during the first few weeks of an online course, instructor-learner interactions may focus heavily on the managerial and technical elements of the course—for example: "I can't log into my class." "How do I get the textbook?" "How do I submit my assignments?" It is important to note that learners will likely have needs that are other than purely pedagogically based.

An instructor who requires students to engage in online discussions should take the time to provide guidelines regarding both the expected quality and quantity of student participation (Kuboni and Martin 2004; Matusov, Hayes, and Pluta 2005). Online class discussions can serve a variety of purposes. Instructors might use a discussion board for student and instructor introductions, class debates, and student-led discussions. This topic will be discussed in much greater detail in regard to student-to-student interaction, but it is worth noting that an instructor's presence in discussions can be very beneficial. A rubric detailing point value distribution will inform students about what is expected and help them understand how they obtained the grade assigned to them.

Instructor presence in discussions can be achieved in a variety of ways. Simply joining the online class discussion is certainly one way of making the instructor's presence known. Another is to provide a summary of the discussions that have taken place and to give feedback on the scope and direction of the discussion. Clarifying and expounding on particular posts, comments, or topics also gives the students an awareness that the instructor is involved in the discussions.

Providing Clear Expectations to Learners

At times online instructors might feel they are overstating the obvious, but providing clear expectations is critical to calming the nerves of even the most veteran online students. In a face-to-face classroom setting, instructors might hand out an assignment and then spend three to five minutes discussing their expectations. It is important not to leave this critical step out of the online learning environment. Although instructors might be tempted to simply use an assignment or activity from a face-to-face course, they should examine the assignment to see if the instructions are clearly laid out for the online student. I have often needed to go back and add quite a bit of additional information for my web-based students.

A veteran online instructor once told me, "Perception is reality." I have often had the feeling that students picture me sitting at my computer twenty-four-hours a day, seven days a week, just waiting to get email from them. I have opened my email account at eight o'clock on a Monday morning to find fifteen emails from a student who sent a first email at midnight on Saturday and just cannot understand why I am not answering. These students are not necessarily upset that I am not answering them; they are stressed and feel disconnected from me. Discussing email and grading response times up front can let students know what to expect and will curtail the anxiety they might feel about not being able to talk face-to-face. For example, I let students know that I will respond to all emails within twenty-four to forty-eight hours, excluding weekends. This assurance reduces their anxiety tremendously.

Letting students know what the timelines are regarding feedback, not only on emails, but also on online forums, assignments, and other interactive activities is imperative. It is not uncommon that students in my courses email me less than twenty-four hours after completing an exam to ask when grades will be posted. Setting expectations in advance helps relieve anxiety. For example, I specify that grades will be posted no later than seven days after the due date of the assignment.

Something as simple as a due date and time can be confusing to students if items are not clearly detailed. For example, if I say that an assignment is due at midnight on Wednesday, will all students agree that midnight is 12:00 a.m. on Wednesday or is it 12:00 a.m. on Tuesday? To make this expectation clearer, I often require items to be due by 11:59 p.m.

Other expectations include details on: (1) how attendance will be taken, (2) honesty policies, (3) no-tolerance policies for rudeness or incivility, (4) homework submitted past the deadline, and (5) grading policies. It has been my experience that providing very detailed information up front reduces the confusion on the students' part and in turn drastically reduces the number of emails to the instructor.

Student-to-Student

Soo and Brush (2008) studied student perceptions of satisfaction in the online environment and discovered that students who perceived high levels of collaborative learning appeared to be more satisfied with their distance education course than those who perceived low levels of collaborative learning. In another study, students reported that the quality of their interactions with other students in web-based courses was similar to those in the traditional classroom setting; they also indicated that the student-to-student interactions were sometimes increased in a web-based course (Lytle, Cross, and Lenhart 2001). Online discussion boards, which give students the opportunity to discuss topics in an open format, afford them an equal voice and also give them time to reflect on the material before supplying a response. The discussion boards also allow for a critical piece of interaction: student-to-student.

Fredericksen et al. (2000) looked at online learning and found that students who reported greater interaction with other students in the course also reported higher levels of learning. Not only do students report a benefit from online discussions, but instructors have also indicated a perceived benefit. Soo and Bonk (1998) reported that online teachers rated the learner-learner interaction as the most important form of interaction.

There are many different types of online discussions. Some instructors use the forum or discussion boards as a place for students to socialize and get to know each other. Others use the platform as a means to allow students to reflect on the material. Still others might have students adding to the group's knowledge base by researching outside resources and bringing relevant discussions back to the online classroom. Another option is to use forum discussions for group presentations and as an opportunity for the students to lead discussions. Whichever techniques (including some that are not addressed here) are used, online discussions provide a connection between students that often separates an online course from a correspondence course. Possibly most importantly, they provide students with the assurance that they are not working through the course alone.

Cox and Cox (2008) also found evidence that interaction between students in the online learning environment can lead to a community of learners. They report that interaction gives the students an opportunity to share thoughts with others in the class. The discussion board creates a collaborative learning environment by allowing students to become acquainted with other students. It also provides a platform for developing networks and rapport between students and instructors. Interestingly, the researchers suggest that the course design does not have to include a separate place for social presence, but rather needs to build the social element into the course design and syllabus. Similarly, it is not the presence of a special social place that establishes meaning and promotes online learning, but rather the design for communication and interaction that are related to social presence and, in turn, to the student's satisfaction in learning (Pate et al. 2009).

Student-to-Interface

Variables that have been linked to learner-interface interactions include computer experience, perceptions about the technology being used, and access to technology. Unfamiliarity with technology has been cited as a potential negative barrier to learning (Schrum and Hong 2002). Students have indicated that their lack of use of technology has resulted in their getting lost in the online environment (Faux and Black-Hughes 2000). Students' perceptions of access to technology also influenced their belief as to whether technology was helpful or inconvenient (Schrum and Hong 2002). Conversely, other students reported that, despite their inexperience with the technology, they felt increased confidence in using a computer by the end of the semester (Billings, Connors, and Skiba 2001; Kenny 2002; Leasure, Davis, and Thievon 2000; Yucha and Princen 2000) and came to view the delays associated with the technology as a time for reflection (Daley et al. 2001). Finally, other studies reported that computer experiences had no impact on overall student satisfaction (Ho, Leong, and Saromines-Ganne 2002; Thurmond et al. 2002).

In essence, the lack of computer experience does not necessarily lead to negative learner-interface interactions. Students who may not be experts in technology may still report positive student outcomes in the course. The key is to address technology issues at the beginning and provide students with the technical support they need not only to access the course but also to research and complete assignments. Having a student-focused technological infrastructure in place is crucial. A customer-focused technical help desk, online demonstration courses, and online student handbooks have proved invaluable resources to me as an online instructor. I also give students a chance to practice using the components of the course by designing short quizzes that simply ask questions about how to use the modules or information provided in the course content sections (i.e., syllabus, student expectations, etc). These quizzes help students address any technical questions that they have before their first "real" course assignment. Also, establishing consistent navigation through the website, notifying students of technical requirements up front, and resisting the use of files that are too big for easy downloading are important considerations that will ease the stress of the less tech-savvy students.

Conclusions

Teaching in the online environment is a very rewarding experience. New online instructors will find that taking the time to address their concerns about connecting with students and providing them with an environment that offers a variety of interactions will only enhance the teaching experience. In turn, the instructors will enhance the learning environment for their students. By addressing student-to-content, student-to-instructor, student-to-student, and student-to-interface connections, instructors can establish an environment that promotes communication and collaborative learning. While this chapter has discussed a variety of tools and techniques to accomplish these goals, by no means is it all-inclusive. As new instructors develop their online classes, innovative ideas are always welcome, and sharing ideas with others in the online learning community will only improve courses for everyone.

References

Berge, Zane L. 1995. "Facilitating Computer Conferencing: Recommendations From the Field." *Educational Technology* 35, no. 1: 22–30.

Billings, Diane M., Helen R. Connors, and Diane J. Skiba. 2001. "Benchmarking Best Practices in Web-Based Nursing Courses." *Advances in Nursing Science* 23: 41–52.

Bonk, Curtis J., Jamie R. Kirkley, Noriko Hara, and Vanessa Dennen. 2001. "Finding the Instructor in Post-Secondary Online Learning: Pedagogical, Social, Managerial, and Technological Locations." In *Teaching and Learning Online: New Pedagogies for New Technologies*, ed. J. Stephenson, 76–97 London: Kogan Page.

Chen, Der-Thanq, Angela F.L. Wong, and Jackie J.-F. Hsu. 2003. "Internet-Based Instructional Activities: Not Everything Should Be on the Internet." *Journal of Research on Technology in Education* 36: 50–59.

Concannon, Fiona, Antoinette Flynn, and Mark Campbell. 2005. "What Campus-Based Students Think About the Quality and Benefits of eLearning." *British Journal of Educational Technology*, 36, no. 3: 501–512.

Conrad, Diane L. 2002. "Engagement, Excitement, Anxiety, and Fear: Learners' Experiences of Starting an Online Course." *Distance Education* 16, no. 4: 205–226.

Cox, Betty, and Becky Cox. 2008. "Developing Interpersonal and Group Dynamics Through Asynchronous Threaded Discussions: The Use of Discussion Boards in Collaborative Learning." *Education* 128, no. 4: 553–565.

Daley, Barbara J., Karen Watkins, Saundra W. Williams, Bradley Courtenay, Mike Davis, and Darryl Dymock. 2001. "Exploring Learning in a Technology-Enhanced Environment." *Educational Technology and Society* 4, no. 3: 126–138.

Darabi, A. Aubteen, Eric G. Sikorski, and Robert G. Harvey. 2006. "Validated Competencies for Distance Teaching." *Distance Education* 27, no. 1: 105–122.

Dennen, Vanessa Paz. 2005. "Task Structuring for On-line Problem Based Learning: A Case Study." *Educational Technology and Society* 3, no. 3: 329–336.

Dennen, Vanessa Paz, A. Aubteen Darabi, and Linda J. Smith. 2007. "Instructor-Learner Interaction in Online Courses: The Relative Perceived Importance of Particular Instructor Actions on Performance and Satisfaction." *Distance Education* 28, no. 1: 65–79.

Faux, Tamara L., and Christine Black-Hughes. 2000. "A Comparison of Using the Internet versus Lectures to Teach Social Work History." *Research on Social Work Practice* 10: 454–466.

Fredericksen, Eric, Alexandra Pickett, William Pelz, Karen Swan, and Peter Shea. 2000. "Student Satisfaction and Perceived Learning with On-line Courses: Principles and Examples from the SUNY Learning Network." *Journal of Asynchronous Learning Networks* 4, no. 2. www.sloanconsortium.org/jaln/v4n2/student-satisfaction-and-perceived-learning-line-courses-principles-and-examples-suny-lear.

Gulbahar, Yasemin, and Soner Yildirim. 2006. "Assessment of Web-Based Courses: A Discussion and Analysis of Learners' Individual Differences and Teaching-learning Process." *International Journal of Instructional Media* 33: 367–378.

Hillman, Daniel C.A., Deborah J. Willis, and Charlotte N. Gunawardena. 1994. "Learner-Interface Interaction in Distance Education: An Extension of Contemporary Models and Strategies for Parishioners." *American Journal of Distance Education* 8, no. 2: 30–42.

Ho, Curtis, Peter Leong, and Barbara Saromines-Ganne. 2002. "An Empirical Investigation of Student Satisfaction with Web-Based Courses." *World Conference on E-Learning in Corporate, Government, Healthcare, and Higher Education, 2002* (1): 1792–1795.

Kenny, Amanda 2002. "Online Learning: Enhancing Nurse Education?" *Journal of Advanced Nursing* 38: 127–135.

Kuboni, Olabisi, and Alicia Martin. 2004. "An Assessment of Support Strategies Used to Facilitate Distance Students' Participation in a Web-Based Learning Environment in the University of the West Indies." *Distance Education* 25, no. 1: 7–29.

Leasure, A. Renee, Lisa Davis, and Susan L. Thievon. 2000. "Comparison of Student Outcomes and Preferences in a Traditional vs. World Wide Web-Based Baccalaureate Nursing Research Course." *Journal of Nursing Education* 39: 149–154.

Lytle, J. Stephen, Carol Cross, and Kevin A. Lenhart. 2001. "Analysis of Large Web-Based Courses at the University of Central Florida." *Society for Informa-*

tion Technology and Teacher Education, International Conference, 2001 (1): 1117–1119.

Matusov, Eugene, Renee Hayes, and Mary Jane Pluta. 2005. "Using a Discussion Web to Develop an Academic Community of Learners." *Educational Technology and Society* 8, no. 2: 16–39.

Moore, Michael G., and Greg Kearsley. 2004. *Distance Education: A Systems View.* 2nd. ed. Belmont, CA: Wadsworth.

Pate, Ardelle, Sharon Smaldino, Hayley J. Mayall, Lara Luetkehans. 2009. "Questioning the Necessity of Nonacademic Social Discussion Forums within Online Courses." *Quarterly Review of Distance Education* 10, no. 1: 1–9.

Russo, Tracy Callaway, and Scott Campbell. 2004. "Perceptions of Mediated Presence in an Asynchronous Online Course: Interplay of Communication Behaviors and Medium." *Distance Education* 25, no. 2: 215–232.

Sanders, Diana W., and Alison I. Morrison-Shetlar. 2001. "Students Attitudes Towards Web-Enhanced Instruction in an Introductory Biology Course." *Journal of Research on Computing in Education* 33: 251–262.

Schrum, Lynne, and Sunjoo Hong. 2002. "Dimensions and Strategies for Online Success: Voices from Experienced Educators." *Journal of Asynchronous Learning Networks* 6, no. 1. www.sloanconsortium.org/jaln/v6n1/dimensions-and-strategies-online-success-voices-experienced-educators.

Soo, Hyo-Jeong, and Thomas A. Brush. 2008. "Student Perceptions of Collaborative Learning, Social Presence and Satisfaction in a Blended Learning Environment: Relationships and Critical Factors." *Computers and Education* 51, no. 1: 318–336.

Soo, Keng-Soon, and Curt J. Bonk. 1998. "Interaction: What Does It Mean in Online Distance Education?" Paper presented at the ED-MEDIA/ED-TELECOM 98 World Conference on Educational Multimedia and Hypermedia and World Conference on Educational Telecommunications (10th), Freiburg, Germany. (ERIC Document Reproduction Service No. ED 428724.)

Swan, Karen. 2001. "Virtual Interaction: Design Factors Affecting Student Satisfaction and Perceived Learning in Asynchronous Online Courses." *Distance Education* 22: 306–331.

Thurmond, Veronica A., Karen Wambach, Helen R. Connors, and Bruce B. Frey. 2002. "Evaluation of Student Satisfaction: Determining the Impact of a Web-Based Environment by Controlling for Student Characteristics." *American Journal of Distance Education* 16: 169–189.

Yucha, Carolyn, and Thomas Princen. 2000. "Insights Learned from Teaching Pathophysiology on the World Wide Web." *Journal of Nursing Education* 39: 68–72.

$\boxed{7}$

Using Social Networking
Applications in Online Teaching

Allen C. Gathman and Mary Harriet Talbut

Teaching online can be a bit like shouting into a cave: you post materials, send emails, and make assignments, then wait for a response. Sometimes it is hard to tell if anyone is out there, much less if you are getting your message across. Students in online courses have the same problem from the other side: they feel isolated. The instructor is a distant presence, and their classmates may not even be detectable. What is lacking in such a situation is a sense of community, of belonging to a group that is engaged in learning. Developing that sense of community can both improve student satisfaction and increase retention in online programs (Joyce and Brown 2009; Rovai 2002). Group work and bulletin boards are examples of tools that instructors can build from the institutional side to promote group interaction and community, but why not come at it from the opposite direction? Chances are that many of your students are engaged with some online social networks already. In addition to trying to bring them to your network, you could go to theirs, capitalizing on the benefits of an existing social structure (Smith et al. 2007). Increasingly, social networks are being used in teaching in academic and corporate settings (Joyce and Brown 2009; Weekes 2008). Another pedagogical advantage of social networking applications is that they contribute to active learning. Instead of using the web as a one-way source of information for the students, these Web 2.0 tools allow the students to take an active role in the online course, fostering constructivist approaches to learning (Virkus 2008).

Definitions of social networking vary; Boyd and Ellison (2007) restrict the term "social network site" to applications that permit users to publish a profile, establish a list of contacts, and view the lists made by their contacts. In this chapter, we consider social networking applications loosely equivalent to Web 2.0, defining them as any web software that allows users to contribute their own content. Social networking would thus include a broad range of tools, including at a minimum instant messaging, blogs, wikis, online games, social networking services, and social bookmarking (Kesim and Agaoglu 2007). The reach of these applications is enormous; for instance, a single social networking service, Facebook, is currently number two in global Internet traffic, behind only Google (Alexa.com 2010). In the following sections of this chapter, we consider Facebook as well as Ning, wikis, blogs, Twitter, social bookmarking, chat, and virtual worlds as possible tools for use in online teaching.

Facebook

If you are looking for your students' online community, you should probably start at Facebook. Facebook is the most popular social networking site in the world, having surpassed MySpace sometime in 2008 (Compete. com 2009); the site reports over 350 million active users (Facebook.com 2010), and its use continues to grow rapidly, in contrast to flat or declining use for its closest rival, MySpace (Alexa.com 2010). Furthermore, since Facebook was originally limited to college students (Boyd and Ellison 2007), it retains an even higher proportional advantage among this audience compared to other such sites. A 2007 survey of Michigan State University students found that 94 percent had Facebook accounts (Ellison, Steinfield, and Lampe 2007). While it is true that use of social networking sites, like other computer skills, varies widely even within the so-called "net generation" (Jones et al. 2009), it is particularly common among college students and probably even more so among those with the technological savvy to be willing to take an online or blended course. There are at least two distinct ways in which a social networking site can augment online teaching. Primarily, it is a way to build a personal connection with students; second, it can be used for substantive interaction about course materials.

Most instructors are aware of the importance of personality in teaching. A significant body of research shows that students have better attitudes toward, and learn better in, classes where instructors share aspects of their personal lives (Cayanus 2004). In the face-to-face classroom, instructors usually do this by joking or digressing briefly from the lecture to mention events in their personal lives. In the online environment, much of this informal interaction is lost, and instructors report feeling that their personality does not come across to the students.

A social networking site such as Facebook provides an easy way for the instructor to "self-disclose," or share personal information. In a 2007 study, Mazer, Murphy, and Simonds found that students had significantly higher expectations for a course taught by an instructor who shared personal information on Facebook compared to one who provided only a photo and academic credentials. Using Facebook in this way requires little from the instructor; you simply need to build a Facebook profile, which is easy using the guidance of the website, and then let your students know that you are on Facebook. You might put a link to your Facebook profile on the course webpage. Students who are curious will look at your profile, and some may ask you to become a "friend."

"Friend" status on Facebook has been written about a great deal recently, and of course it is not the same as traditional friendship. You may choose not to accept current students as friends, thus limiting their access to the public parts of your profile. On the other hand, you may accept students as friends, but limit their access via the privacy settings. With the highly customizable privacy controls now available, Facebook makes it possible to carefully regulate what personal information you share.

Facebook Privacy Settings

One way of managing contact with students on Facebook is to create a friends list for current students. If you click on **friends** in Facebook, you will see a list of all your friends, along with a button labeled **create new list**. One of the authors of this chapter made a list called "current students" and put all current students into it. Next you can define the access that this group of friends will have. Click on **settings** and choose **manage privacy**. Then select **profile information**. Here you find a list of all the information you have put in your profile, including **personal info**, **religious and political views**, **photo albums**, and other material.

Suppose you want to keep your religious and political views private from your students: click on the button at the end of that line and choose **customize**. You will see a box saying **make this visible to** and **hide this from**. You can choose to make those views visible to friends, but hide them from the **current students** list. You can manage privacy for all the parts of your profile from this page. You can even set privacy settings for individual photo albums—for instance, you can allow your students to see "Bob and Sue's Wedding," but not "Bob's Bachelor Party."

Privacy settings are particularly important for faculty who have had Facebook profiles for some time. A study at a large U.S. university, for instance, indicated that many medical students and residents included publicly accessible information and photos in their Facebook profiles that gave an unprofessional impression (Ferdig et al. 2008). Students in other fields may well be similar, and thus new faculty should probably give some attention to choosing appropriate privacy settings. Although you can delete any information you put on Facebook, once it has been online, it is always possible that someone has it cached somewhere and so starting with appropriate privacy settings is safer.

In summary, with judicious choice of privacy settings, a Facebook profile can give your students a glimpse of your no doubt winning personality and thus improve their attitudes toward coursework and their willingness to communicate with you about the course.

Facebook Chat

In fact, the Facebook chat feature can provide a direct line of communication. Students in our classes who are our Facebook friends frequently ask questions about coursework using chat—particularly when an exam is coming up soon. When we first encountered this feature, we made a point of mentioning it in class and inviting all students to friend us and make use of the feature. It is probably best to make the suggestion publicly so as not to exclude anyone from this potential means of communicating. Of course, this is synchronous communication, and by its nature it may exclude students whose schedules differ widely from yours.

Facebook Groups and Fan Pages

Facebook can also provide more formal opportunities for group and community interaction in an online class. Two possible forums for course-related material are Facebook groups and Facebook fan pages. Both of these provide a sort of "membership," either by joining the group or by becoming a "fan." Both forums show up on your profile page (assuming you make that information accessible). Both have a wall, a discussion feature, and photos. Both, in essence, provide community space for your students to collaborate and share ideas, links, photos, and so on. Both provide an opportunity for your students to be "introduced" to each other on Facebook, as they will see other students listed as members and may choose to friend them. These features also provide another possible advantage over your personal Facebook profile; your students can share ideas with you and each other on one of these pages without being your (or each other's) Facebook friends. If you (or your students) are particularly concerned over privacy issues, groups or fan pages may be a way to make use of the Facebook network while maintaining a high degree of privacy.

There are two main differences between group and fan pages. First, anyone not specifically banned by the page administrator can become a fan of a page; groups can be open, or open only by invitation, or private. Second, posts to a group show up only on the group page. Posts to a fan page show up in the live feed of every fan.

What does this mean in practice? A group is useful if you have mo-tivated students who are going to seek out the group page on a regular basis to receive or provide information. It can be useful to have a group for a particular course if you are going to require students to use it for some purpose. Also, if the material you plan to put on the group page is not for public dissemination, this is the best choice. But remember, when you post something on the group page, the only way students will know about it is if they intentionally seek out the page and look at it. You have to consider all the demands on your students' time and decide whether they will actually do this.

A fan page, on the other hand, calls your students' attention to itself every time someone adds something to it. If you are planning to use the page as a supplement, to foster discussion or share materials above and beyond the course requirements, this is probably the best choice. When you put up that great link to an online article on your course's fan page, every student who is a fan and who looks at Facebook that day will know about it. You can also buy paid ads for a fan page, so if you want to promote enrollment in a class, you can pay for Facebook to run ads on the Facebook pages of students at your institution.

Whether you use a group or a fan page, it is a good idea to post a clear set of rules for conduct, covering what kinds of materials may be posted, whether any topics or behaviors are prohibited, and so on. In both types of pages, you have some control. You can choose whether fans or members may write on the wall, post photos, post videos, and post links. As administrator of your group or page, you can ban specific individuals if necessary. In our experience, a fan page, where timely supplemental information can be posted, is a useful adjunct to a course.

Ning

Ning (www.ning.com) is an online platform that enables people or groups to create their own social network. As stated earlier, both students and instructors in an online class may have a sense of isolation and disconnect, as if they are "shouting in a cave." By creating a classroom Ning, they can enjoy the benefits of a social network but on a more intimate scale. In a face-to-face course, students meet in the hall or some other place before or after class meetings; a Ning can act as the place where online students meet. Depending upon your own school's technology capabilities, the Ning could be the place where videos can be posted and group work planned. According to Crystal Beach (2009), who uses a Ning as a teacher and student, it is less cumbersome and allows for more collaboration than the course management systems some schools use. As the semesters go on, new students can be added to the class Ning and former students who are working in the field can be contacted to connect with the class, building a professional network.

Wikis

While a fan page on Facebook provides a shared space where students can post information of interest, the structure of the page limits its usefulness. To collaboratively produce and share large amounts of material in an organized way, a wiki is probably the best option. A wiki is a website that allows users to create, edit, and interlink webpages directly from a standard web browser program. The online encyclopedia Wikipedia is the best-known wiki, but private or limited-access wikis are in use in a wide variety of educational, avocational, and corporate settings.

The great strength of a wiki is that it provides a repository of information that is fully collaborative, fostering active learning in an online environment (Reynard 2009). Every student may be an author; knowledge is not solely invested in a textbook or instructor, but constructed by a learning community. From a practical standpoint, it allows the instructor to view the process of revision in its entirety and to assess the role of each student, as all revisions and their authors are preserved in the page histories. It can also provide a continually updated resource for a course, incorporating new information in a more timely fashion than is possible with a print text.

Setting Up a Wiki

The first choice to be made is between hosting a wiki on an institutional server and making use of an online platform. Free wiki platforms include Google Sites (http://sites.google.com), Wikispaces (www.wikispaces.com), and Wikidot (www.wikidot.com). All of these allow construction of wikis on public servers, with varying levels of control over access and amounts of storage available. Setting up a wiki on any of these free platforms is relatively easy and user-friendly, with copious online help available.

If you have instructional technology (IT) support that will permit you to construct a wiki on an institutional server, this route allows for more control over access, more freedom in customizing the site, and (usually) more storage space. A huge array of software packages, many of them free and open source, is available for use on your server; the relevant Wikipedia entry gives a good analysis of the strengths and weaknesses of each. Installing the software and starting a wiki using one of these packages is best left to the IT staff, but once the wiki is up and running, creating and editing pages is straightforward.

The variety of software packages makes it prohibitive to present step-by-step instructions for creating and editing wiki pages here. In general, wiki programs allow page creation and editing either using a fairly intuitive, "word processor-like" editor (WYSIWYG—"what you see is what you get"), or a text-based markup language similar to HTML code. The latter is used in MediaWiki, the platform on which Wikipedia is based, and the vast number of Wikipedia contributors is testament that markup language editors are not difficult to learn. In any case, all the available packages offer plenty of online help to which you and your students can refer.

Guidelines

The wiki format is so endlessly adaptable that it is necessary to set some standards from the start to avoid growing an amorphous monster. You need to think about what you want the wiki to be and make that clear from the start. From experience, here are some points to consider:

- Make sure the goal of the wiki is clear, and communicate its purpose to your class—for example, building a resource for future classes or building a resource to help class members study for the final.
- Decide who the audience will be—the current class, future classes, outsiders, and so on.
- Identify a moderator/editor who will ensure that contributions fit the goal and format. This needs to be some responsible person—usually the instructor of the class if the members will move on.
- Provide clear instructions on how to use the wiki and how to contribute. Many times the hardest part is signing up because most students are unfamiliar with the process. It is best to give an introductory assignment early in the course in which students simply have to sign on and make some minimal contribution.
- Promote a culture of friendly collaboration in the wiki.

The collaborative process of creating a wiki does not happen automatically. As with any assignment, working on the wiki competes with many other demands on students' time. Thus it is important to set clear goals and deadlines for specific outcomes: for instance, a page on a selected topic with a certain amount of content by a certain date. Reynard (2009) recommends a framework from a business model known as SMSM:

1. Scope out: define the scope of a project, including both the students to be working on it and the area it will cover.
2. Map out: in collaboration with students, name each project appropriately.
3. Stake out: let students brainstorm resources and time that will be needed.
4. Measure out: set specific timelines and outcomes.

Reynard also suggests that instructors should provide feedback during the process by occasionally identifying a particularly noteworthy contribution and asking its author to explain the thought process involved.

Examples

The adaptability of the wiki format means that its applications are limited primarily by your (and your students') imagination. Instructors report using wikis in a wide variety of ways (Mader 2006; Smart Teaching 2008; West and West 2009).

The most obvious use is collaborative construction of a course-specific reference, a sort of focused "mini-Wikipedia." One of the authors uses a wiki as the textbook for a genetics course, with pages constructed and edited by students. Students gain a sense of ownership of the course material and of responsibility for each other's learning by creating such a resource, and they may be able to identify study tips or solution strategies that are particular to the class. You may require students to document their information, thus helping them to connect knowledge to its sources in research. Ideally, constructing such a resource should give students practice in techniques of locating and gathering information that will serve them well beyond the college years.

A wiki is also an easy way for students to construct webpages, presentations, or written work collaboratively. If group assignments are stored in the wiki, then each member's contribution is readily apparent, older versions can be readily restored if needed, and the work is always available to the whole group—no danger that the student who had the file will be sick on the day of the presentation. The wiki can also be used for peer editing of individual papers or simply for students to draft, revise, and polish their own writing.

In research, wikis are frequently used for data collection. One of us lets the students construct the class roll by signing on to the wiki and adding their names to the list. In a similar fashion, if students are conducting multiple replications of an experiment, each student or group can report data into a wiki page, where it is immediately collected for the use of the whole class.

Wikis lend themselves readily to making lists of any sort, since individuals may contribute discrete items to one. If students find links to websites, images, or videos relevant to course material, they can easily add them to a wiki page for future reference. Similarly, a glossary of terms and definitions is easy to construct and provides an opportunity for each student to contribute something.

Each content page in a wiki also has a discussion page. Students may be encouraged to use the discussion pages for outlining, proposing revisions to collaborative work, or arguing over contentious points. The discussion pages themselves provide another sort of online community where students interact with each other on relevant issues.

The great strength of a wiki, that it allows all users to be authors, is also its weakness: wiki content tends to be choppy and lack synthesis and integration. As Reynard (2009) points out, the instructor should resist the urge to take over the role of editor. Students can develop valuable skills in synthesis by working to find connections and themes, then revising content to reflect them. This higher-order skill, of course, must be fostered by giving students clear responsibilities and timelines for this sort of work.

Blogs

A blog (shortened from "web log") is a more linear online community application, in which one or several individuals can post entries, and readers may comment on them. Blogs have proliferated greatly in recent years, particularly those devoted to specific topics as a form of journalism. Research indicates that relatively few students actually have a personal blog, however, so this platform may not be as familiar to them as some others (Kennedy et al. 2007). Many students may be using the notes feature in Facebook in lieu of a formal blog.

In the classroom, a blog may offer an intermediate point between completely instructor-centered course materials and completely student-generated materials such as wiki content. The instructor may post on a topic and then ask students to provide responses as comments. On the other hand, all students may have posting access, in which case the blog becomes similar to a course discussion bulletin board, like those provided by most online course management systems.

Several free sites host blogs, including Blogger (www.blogger.com), WordPress (http://wordpress.com), and LiveJournal (www.livejournal. com). Blogs also may be hosted on institutional servers, and, as suggested above, most blog functions can probably be accomplished using online course management software.

Microblogging

Microblogging is a form of multimedia blogging that allows users to publish brief text updates or micromedia such as photos or audio clips to be viewed either by anyone or by a restricted group chosen by the user. These messages can be submitted by a variety of means, including text messaging, instant messaging, email, digital audio, or the web. The content of a microblog differs from a traditional blog in that it is typically smaller in actual size and aggregate file size. A single entry could consist of a single sentence or fragment, an image, or a brief, ten-second video. But its purpose is similar to that of a traditional blog. The microblogging function could be accomplished using online course management software or a place established on the course website where announcements are posted.

Twitter

Twitter is a free social networking and microblogging service that enables its users to send and read messages known as *tweets*. These updates are limited to a maximum of 140 characters. Senders can restrict delivery to those in their circle of friends or, by default, allow open access. Users can send and receive tweets via the Twitter website, short message service (SMS), or external applications. While the service itself costs nothing to use, accessing it through SMS may incur phone service provider fees. Other users may search for tweets by subject or choose to follow a particular user's tweets and receive them when the user updates. Although it has become notorious as a repository of trivia about users' daily lives, Twitter may be used in professional and educational contexts as well.

Students could follow the instructor using an individual or a Twitter account set up strictly for class purposes; the instructor could use tweets to give short updates or reminders to the class. Research shows that real-time communication, such as live chat and prompt feedback on assignments, is associated with perceived "immediacy" in online courses and thus with community formation and student satisfaction (Woods and Ebersole 2003). It seems likely that tweets, sent and received via cell phone, could provide one form of immediate communication to achieve this goal.

Twitter can be as useful or important as the people it is used to follow. For example, Twitter can be used to create a personal learning network (PLN). One of the authors has learned many Web 2.0 tools for teaching by using Twitter to follow other instructors who tweet links to sites or blogs of interest. Tom Whitby (2009) at St. Joseph's College of Education in New York requires his students to create a Twitter account so they can begin to build a PLN that will continue to enhance their learning in professional life.

Yammer (www.yammer.com) is a similar application that provides a secure controlled-access microblogging platform with the same 140-character limit. As it is not public, it may be preferable for applications where privacy is important. This could transform an online class of isolated students into a rich network of approachable contacts. As discussions grow to include questions, content links, and information dissemination, content can be searched and serve as a knowledge base for the class.

Social Bookmarking

Delicious (http://delicious.com), Digg (http://digg.com), and Stumble-Upon (www.stumbleupon.com) are all platforms for what is known broadly as "social bookmarking." These applications allow you to tag a website that you like and append a brief comment or review. Other users can follow your bookmarks, seeing a list of the sites you like and your comments about them.

In the classroom, you can invite students to follow your social bookmarks as a means of distributing web links to them. To be more collaborative, you can follow your students as well, encouraging them to tag sites that are relevant to the course. Social bookmarking thus provides a way to share content interactively, with contributions from both instructor and students.

Chat

Various platforms, including AIM (http://products.aim.com), Google Talk (www.google.com/talk), Facebook, and some online course management systems, allow live chat. Live chat with scheduled "office hours" is one way to increase immediacy in the online environment, giving students a sense of personal contact with the instructor (Woods and Ebersole 2003). One drawback is that, in an asynchronous course, not all students may be able to make use of a synchronous communication method such as chat, perhaps leading some students to feel like outsiders. One possible solution is to archive the chats and post them so that they are available to all students; this is easy with Google Talk, for instance. When teaching via webinar, one author has found the chat feature of the course delivery system to be the most efficient form of communication between students and instructor during online class meetings.

Virtual Worlds

A virtual world is an online environment where users are represented by 3D images or "avatars" that can interact in a graphic environment and make and use virtual objects. The most widely known of these virtual worlds is Second Life. Numerous university educators make use of Second Life as an online teaching environment, particularly useful for group interaction and display of three-dimensional models (Cook 2009; Sussman 2007). A full treatment of the use of virtual worlds in education is beyond the scope of this chapter; several wikis document educational uses of Second Life (Jokaydia.com 2010; Second Life 2010; Simteach 2010), and there is an extensive online annotated bibliography (Pepper 2010).

Final Thoughts

The large number of applications available may seem daunting, but their modular nature allows the instructor to try one at a time and approach social networking gradually. Most important, the tool must serve a clear educational goal. This may simply be fostering community and affective learning, or it may include content and skills as well. Clearly conceptualizing the goals in advance and sharing them with the students is essential. When students know the goal, they can then suggest how they could or already do use the tool to make achievement of that goal a reality.

One important consideration in using web applications is the diversity of student backgrounds. There has been considerable recent attention to the so-called "Net generation" (Tapscott 2008), and we are often admonished that our students expect revolutionary change in instructional methods (Palfrey and Gasser 2008; Virkus 2008). As Marc Prensky (2001) said, "today's students *think and process information fundamentally differently* from their predecessors." However, empirical studies show that the reach of Web 2.0 is not as broad as is sometimes imagined (Kennedy et al. 2007) and that students fall into diverse groups rather than a monolithic "digital generation" (Jones et al. 2009).

Although online students are likely to group near the high end of the spectrum for computer knowledge, not every student will be familiar with the tools you choose to use in class. At the risk of boring the computer-savvy, be sure to make step-by-step instructions available to all the students, and start any Web 2.0 venture with an icebreaker assignment in order to verify that everyone is able to log on and use the tool. Students may know one particular social network program really well, but have limited if any knowledge of other Web 2.0 tools. The learning curve may not be steep, but you do need to provide time for that curve. Videotaped instructions on how to use the basics of the Web 2.0 tool or program may be saved on the course website where other class resources are found. These can provide a safety net for students and ease communication issues for the instructor. In addition, if possible, links to examples created by students from previous semesters (and used with their permission) can be included on the course resource page.

One important issue: students have a lot of demands on their time. In some situations, students who are highly motivated will participate in class social networking on their own, but often you will need to provide them with some motivation. The currency of academia is credit, of course, and in our experience, if you want students to participate actively, you will probably need to award credit for doing so. Typically, we construct several assignments for any new online tool. First, an ice-breaker, as mentioned before, that requires students simply to log on and perform some token task. Subsequent assignments give students more responsibility for content development, such as adding to an existing wiki page or commenting on a blog post. After such simple tasks, students can be given responsibility for yet more substantive contributions, often in collaboration with others in a group. Prompt feedback and constructive suggestions are important in maintaining the immediacy of the online environment. Scoring guides for major projects are a must, as the "wide openness" of social networks and Web 2.0 tool assignments can be overwhelming to some students. The guides provide direction and clarity by helping students understand how the instructor grades their work.

Any pedagogical technology, from chalk to virtual reality, is of course only a tool rather than an end in itself. We have suggested here some possibilities, but the flexibility of Web 2.0 tools and social networking sites ensures that the list can never be exhaustive. Your experience and imagination will be the best guides. The important thing is to start with clearly defined goals, to make those goals clear to the students, and to provide the students with support throughout the process. Then be willing to listen to any suggestions from the students that will make their educational experiences better. When you are finished with the assignment or lesson, a good reflective question to ask is: "Did the technology make the lesson better?" If the answer is no, adjust your pedagogy so that the answer is yes the next time.

References

Alexa.com. 2010. "Facebook.com—Site Info From Alexa." www.alexa.com/siteinfo/facebook.com.

Beach, Crystal. 2009. Personal communication.

Boyd, Danah M., and Nicole B. Ellison. 2007. "Social Network Sites: Definition, History, and Scholarship." *Journal of Computer Mediated Communication—Electronic Edition* 13, no. 1: 210.

Cayanus, Jacob L. 2004. "Effective Instructional Practice: Using Teacher Self-Disclosure as an Instructional Tool." *Communication Teacher* 18, no. 1: 6–9.

Compete.com. 2009. "Social Networks: Facebook Takes Over Top Spot, Twitter Climbs." February 9. http://blog.compete.com/2009/02/09/facebook-myspace-twitter-social-network/.

Cook, Ann D. 2009. "A Case Study of the Manifestations and Significance of Social Presence in a Multi-User Virtual Environment." MA thesis, University of Saskatchewan.

Ellison, Nicole B., Charles Steinfield, and Cliff Lampe. 2007. "The Benefits of Facebook 'Friends': Social Capital and College Students' Use of Online Social Network Sites." http://jcmc.indiana.edu/v0112/issue4/ellison.html.

Facebook.com. 2010. "Facebook | Statistics." www.facebook.com/press/info.php?statistics.

Ferdig, Richard E., Kara Dawson, Erik W. Black, Nicole M. Paradise Black, and Lindsay A. Thompson. 2008. "Medical Students' and Residents' Use of Online Social Networking Tools: Implications for Teaching Professionalism in Medical Education." September 1. http://firstmonday.org/htbin/cgiwrap/bin/ojs/index.php/fm/article/view/2161/2026.

Jokaydia.com. 2010. "Jokaydia: Exploring Virtual Worlds." http://wiki.jokaydia.com/page/Main_Page.

Jones, Chris, Ruslan Ramanau, Simon Cross, and Graham Healing. 2009. "Net Generation or Digital Natives: Is There a Distinct New Generation Entering University?" *Computers & Education* 54, no. 3, Learning in Digital Worlds: Selected Contributions from the CAL 09 Conference, April 2010, pp. 722–732. www.sciencedirect.com/science/article/B6VCJ-4XFXSPS-2/2/8c4e9ee1734216b2ab14544598ab5c67).

Joyce, Kristopher M., and Abbie Brown. 2009. "Enhancing Social Presence in Online Learning: Mediation Strategies Applied to Social Networking Tools." www.westga.edu/~distance/ojdla/winter124/joyce124.html.

Kennedy, Gregor, Barney Dalgarno, Kathleen Gray, Terry Judd, Jenny Waycott, Susan Bennett, Karl Maton, et al. 2007. "The Net Generation Are Not Big Users of Web 2.0 Technologies: Preliminary Findings." ICT: Providing Choices for Learners and Learning. Proceedings Ascilite Singapore. www.ascilite.org.au/conferences/singapore07/procs/kennedy.pdf.

Kesim, Eren, and Esmahan Agaoglu. 2007. "A Paradigm Shift in Distance Education: Web 2.0 and Social Software." http://tojde.anadolu.edu.tr/tojde27/articles/article_4.htm.

Mader, Stewart. 2006. "Using Wiki in Education | Future Changes." October 24. www.ikiw.org/education/.

Mazer, Joseph, Richard Murphy, and Cheri Simonds. 2007. "I'll See You On 'Facebook': The Effects of Computer-Mediated Teacher Self-Disclosure on Student Motivation, Affective Learning, and Classroom Climate." *Communication Education* 56, no. 1: 1–17.

Palfrey, John, and Urs Gasser. 2008. *Born Digital: Understanding the First Generation of Digital Natives.* New York: Basic Books.

Pepper, Mark. 2010. "Bibliography of Second Life Education." http://web.ics. purdue.edu/~mpepper/slbib.

Prensky, Marc. 2001. "Digital Natives, Digital Immigrants." www.twitchspeed. com/site/Prensky%20-%20Digital%20Natives,%20Digital%20Immigrants%20 -%20Part1.htm.

Reynard, Ruth. 2009. "More Challenges With Wikis: 4 Ways to Move Students from Passive to Active." *THE Journal*, October 7. http://thejournal.com/ articles/2009/10/07/more-challenges-with-wikis-4-ways-to-move-students-from-passive-to-active.aspx.

Rovai, Alfred P. 2002. "Building Sense of Community at a Distance." *International Review of Research in Open and Distance Learning* 3, no. 1: 1–16.

Second Life. 2010. "Education—Second Life Wiki." http://wiki.secondlife.com/ wiki/Education.

Simteach. 2010. "Second Life Education Wiki–SimTeach." www.simteach.com/ wiki/index.php?title=Second_Life_Education_Wiki.

Smart Teaching. 2008. "50 Ways to Use Wikis for a More Collaborative and Interactive Classroom." August 4. www.smartteaching.org/blog/2008/08/50-ways-to-use-wikis-for-a-more-collaborative-and-interactive-classroom/.

Smith, Carter F., Gary F. Schneider, George Kontos, Hanan Kuzat, James Janossy, Karen Thurmond, Beth Moore, Lynn Whitledge, Priscilla Speer, Annette Harber, et al. 2007. "Engaging the Learner." 12th Annual Instructional Technology Conference, Murfreesboro, Tennessee, April 1–3, online submission, 190.

Sussman, Beth. 2007. "Teachers, College Students Lead a Second Life—USATODAY.com." August 1. www.usatoday.com/news/education/2007-08-01-second-life_N.htm.

Tapscott, Don. 2008. *Grown Up Digital: How the Net Generation Is Changing Your World.* New York: McGraw-Hill.

Virkus, Sirje. 2008. "Use of Web 2.0 Technologies in LIS Education: Experiences at Tallinn University, Estonia." *Program: Electronic Library and Information Systems* 42, no. 3: 262–274.

Weekes, Sue. 2008. "E-learning on the Social." *Training & Coaching Today* (November–December): 15.

West, James A., and Margaret L. West. 2009. *Using Wikis for Online Collaboration: The Power of the Read-Write Web.* San Francisco: Jossey-Bass.

Whitby, Thomas. 2009. Personal communication.

Woods, Robert, and Samuel Ebersole. 2003. "Becoming a 'Communal Architect' in the Online Classroom: Integrating Cognitive and Affective Learning for Maximum Effect in Web-Based Learning." www.westga.edu/%7Edistance/ojdla/ spring61/woods61.htm.

8

Redirecting Discussion

Challenges Related to the Social Aspects of Online Educational Environments

Melanie L. Buffington

I was relieved to see that someone finally responded to what I had posted a few days earlier. Though I started reading the graduate student's post quickly about how he teaches students to draw faces, I slowed down as I came across the words Negroid, Caucasoid, and Mongoloid. How could he not know how offensive those words were? I double-checked that I was not overreacting by Googling the words he used, and, as I suspected, they were all used on hate group websites.

What was this student trying to convey in his post? What was I, as the teacher, supposed to do? Emailing him individually to discuss the issue would protect his privacy, but if I did not address this issue publicly, my silence would be a tacit endorsement of his language and ideas. However, I did not want to berate him in front of everyone in the class. I had no way to know who had already read his post or who might read a response that I could post to the class blog. Not knowing what else to do, I quickly emailed a few friends to get their thoughts on how to handle the situation.

At the heart of this chapter is the issue of students posting incorrect, inappropriate, or insensitive comments in online education forums, and to explore options for dealing with them. The use of inappropriate and insensitive language in classrooms is certainly not a new topic in education. However, the widespread use of online educational environments raises new possibilities for how inappropriate language may manifest itself.[1] Though similar issues arise in face-to-face classrooms, online environments present unique challenges.

In addition to dealing with inappropriate student comments, I address strategies for helping students monitor posts and for managing the volume of posts. Discussion boards, blogs, chat, live classroom, and other technologies allow for significant social interaction online. The social nature of learning is an important aspect of online teaching and learning. Through a review of relevant literature interspersed with anecdotes from my online teaching, my students' ideas, and the experiences of friends and colleagues, I offer several suggestions for dealing with these issues.[2] They are meant not as prescriptive solutions, but rather as a means to begin a dialogue within education about how these issues are similar to and different from issues that instructors encounter in face-to-face teaching.

Relevant Literature

There is certainly an abundant amount of literature on teaching online in various settings. The literature addresses topics as diverse as the technical aspects of online teaching, cost-benefit analyses of online classes, gender issues in online courses, and the effectiveness of online courses, among numerous other topics. The literature on online environments places a great deal of emphasis upon how to structure the online environment of a course. Certainly, course management tools require a significant investment of time to learn how to use the software and how to structure the course. Less often emphasized is the sense of community and the type of human interactions that may take place online. This approach to learning, based upon the myriad aspects of constructivism, is as important as the technical aspects of the course. Constructivism is an educational philosophy that posits that the learner constructs knowledge rather than being the recipient of knowledge delivered by the teacher (Vygotsky 1978). Social interactions among students are widely viewed as a crucial part of the learning process from a constructivist viewpoint. However, facilitating constructivist learning through social interactions and developing a positive class culture may not be the same online as they are in face-to-face classrooms. In the literature on this narrower topic, two main themes emerge: the need to reconsider theories of education in light of online learning (Burbules 2004; Mishra and Juwah 2006; Simonson et al. 2003; Sims and Hedberg 2006; Waterhouse 2005) and the importance of social interactions in online learning environments (Dyke et al. 2007; Palloff and Pratt 2003, 2007; Pegrum 2007; Waterhouse 2005). I discuss these themes in the following sections as they relate to various scenarios that I encountered in online teaching.

Social Interactions Online

There is no widely agreed upon description of what constitutes a social interaction that is likely to lead to learning in an online or face-to-face course. For the purpose of this chapter, I argue that there are at least three forms of student responses relating to online communication options in online courses: task completion, neutral interactions, and meaningful interactions. A task completion response refers to students who mainly interact with the technology and merely post something related to the question being asked. These types of posts do not respond to or relate to other student or teacher posts. These students do not engage with others and may seem to be "talking at" the group rather than interacting with the group. In a neutral interaction response, a student responds to another person, either student or teacher, but the post merely reinforces what a student believes and does not challenge, question, or push the thinking process. An example of a neutral interaction occurs when a student posts a comment on a discussion board and another student responds by saying "Good idea" or "I agree." Additionally, a neutral interaction may involve a student offering a story to reinforce what another student posted. For instance, if one student shares a story related to a point in the readings and another student commends that student for making a connection, that would be a neutral interaction. Though these students are interacting socially, they are not doing so in ways that are likely to build new knowledge or to push themselves to think about why they hold the beliefs that they do. However, these types of interactions may build a social relationship between and among students that can later lead to meaningful interactions. In contrast, a meaningful interaction is characterized by some type of exchange that challenges students to think in a new way, to question what they previously believed, or to defend a position that they presented to the class. Though all three types of posts might be common in an online class, it is the neutral and meaningful interactions that engage students in discussion and build a sense of community.

Suggestions for Creating Class Culture in an Online Course

Just as a productive positive culture does not inherently emerge in a face-to-face course, it does not inherently happen in an online course. Like the first efforts of many other online instructors, my initial foray into using online elements in teaching was not preceded by coursework or training in the area.

In response to student needs, I implemented a course structure that utilized a blog in an attempt to make the course more convenient for the students. The following year, I taught my first fully online course using a course management system that was new to me. The training provided by my university focused on the functional aspects of the technology, including the visual interface, file upload system, gradebook application, and how the system related to the other university-wide computing systems. Like many new online teachers, I focused on the most immediate concern of learning to use the technology and gave little thought to the social and community-building aspects of the course. Over the next five years of teaching a variety of other classes completely or partially online, I developed strategies to manage the social aspects of online courses. On the following pages, I describe some of the situations that I have encountered and some of the strategies that my colleagues and I have developed to handle them.

Scenario: Students do not interact with each other online, mainly "talk at" each other, and are not building knowledge and understanding together.

The vast majority of my students in online course are teachers who are earning master's degrees while they teach full-time. This puts a significant limitation on the amount of time they allocate for their coursework. After my first experience with the class utilizing a blog, I realized that the students were mainly talking at each other rather than interacting with each other. My best guess is that they were making the minimum number of required posts per week in the most efficient manner—by posting their ideas and not reading and responding to the ideas of others.

This realization led me to rethink my assumptions about teaching and learning in an online environment. There are numerous theories relevant to distance education, online education, and elearning (Simonson et al. 2003). To effectively teach in an online environment, it is essential that instructors rethink their pedagogical methods (Burbules 2004; Mishra and Juwah 2006; Waterhouse 2005). Sims and Hedberg (2006) argue that online classes may be structured on the basis of existing theories that are predicated on face-to-face models of education. However, successful online learning strategies do more than merely take a face-to-face model and put it online. Instead, they must be adapted from the face-to-face models or created to suit the online learning environment. Burbules (2004) notes that when materials and methods are merely taken from the physical classroom and digitized, opportunities for learning might be lost. Additionally, Sims and Hedberg (2006) believe that certain technical aspects of course management systems may impede the development of interactivity in an online course. They also discuss the need to socialize the students into the culture of the online course. Haythornthwaite et al. (2004, 35) mention the shift in online learning to actively facilitate the development of community among the learners in a particular course. They note the importance of developing robust online courses and not letting them merely be electronic correspondence courses: "Key to overcoming the correspondence model is moving the students from the position of an isolated learner to that of a member of a learning community."

Though the term "instructional delivery" or other variations of the concept may be used in literature relating to online learning (Waterhouse 2005), other scholars do not agree that this term is an appropriate way to conceive of online learning. Burbules (2004, 5) writes that the technologies associated with online learning are not "a 'delivery system' for course content (a ridiculous conception of teaching in any event, since teaching is not about the *delivery* of information)." Palloff and Pratt (1999) express a similar belief and indicate that the relationships people develop and the interactions among them are important ways learning occurs. As these relationships and interactions are different online than in face-to-face classroom settings, they need to be considered within the context of an online environment rather than conceived of as the delivery of instruction.

My readings in this area led me to change the ways I had students interacting online. The first shift I tried involved assigning two levels of responses for each week's readings, primary and secondary responses. The primary responses were for students to answer the open-ended discussion questions and to show that they had read and understood the week's assigned readings. The secondary responses were for students to respond to each other's posts and question, challenge, and support each other. After encouraging students to interact socially through the discussion board, I found it difficult to wade through all the social conversations when grading their posts. Thus, I began including an ungraded space on the discussion board titled "The Lounge" where students could interact as they might before and after a face-to-face class, checking on each other, sharing ideas related to their teaching, asking for suggestions on handling their own students, and so on.

After working with the strategy of primary and secondary responses for a few semesters, I found that many students had similar primary responses; such uniformity did not further the discussion. I therefore expanded this strategy by dividing the class into four-person groups and assigning a specific role for each group member in the online discussion forum; a different group of students led the discussion each week. The following four roles forced the students outside of their comfort zones and pushed the discussion into a variety of directions:

- Provocateur—devil's advocate who poses provocative questions
- Connector—find relationships between and among student posts and articles
- Resister—does not believe the methodology or reading is important; pokes holes in the arguments of the authors
- Champion—sees the merit of the methodology or the article and argues for its importance

Not only did this strategy make the forum interactions more interesting, it encouraged the group leading the discussion to take more ownership of the material. This led to a stronger sense of community among all the groups as they often met virtually outside of the forum to plan their discussion and how they would mediate their classmates' responses.

When I discussed the issue of building community in an online course with colleagues and friends, they offered additional suggestions. One colleague suggested holding a few face-to-face class meetings during the semester and also sending periodic provocative emails to the group with encouragement and commentary about the course discussions (McKay 2007). Another colleague suggested allowing students an opportunity to speak about themselves and their lives in a dialogical format related to the class discussion. She also has students post and discuss their own and other students' writing assignments. Both of these suggestions allow students to develop a sense of who their peers are and what topics interest them, thus resulting in a stronger bond among the students in the class (Lai 2007).

Scenario: Students in an online class make more than 150 posts per week and the professor simply cannot read and respond to all of them.

It is very likely that the professor may not be able to read and respond to all posts every week. In my online classes, the number of posts per week typically ranges between 125 and 175. Though I do my best, I cannot always read and comment on them all in a timely manner. Also, a professor who responds to all messages reinforces a hierarchical class structure rather than one in which multiple voices are valued. Thus, it is important that the professor and students share the responsibility to address issues in the posts. Based upon my reading, I implemented several strategies that relieved the overload and simultaneously increased my students' interest in the course content.

Edelstein and Edwards (2002) explore the idea that interactions online enable students to build their knowledge of the course content and make connections to their lives beyond the course. The authors offer several suggestions to build social interactions that are conducive to learning when designing course assignments utilizing threaded discussions. They say that the question needs to be phrased appropriately, that students need to receive feedback, and that students may need redirection or encouragement to make their participation on the discussion board a meaningful learning experience.

Building upon the work of Edelstein and Edwards (2002), I changed the types of questions that I was asking, allowed students more choices in their responses, and found ways to increase the feedback that they received. Specifically, I wrote more questions that allowed them to build connections between the weekly readings and their individual research interests. I also posted a greater number of questions, but allowed students to answer a set number of them. For instance, I might post six questions and require students to pick the three that most interested them for their responses. For the second round of responses, I would ask students to respond to each other on the same question. Thus, they would give and receive feedback relating to a question that they were able to choose. This strategy allowed me to focus my reading and responses on the students who did not receive feedback from their peers. This reduced the time I spent giving feedback and simultaneously gave students more control over their own learning and built more connections between them.

Scenario: A student makes a post to a discussion board that is not correct.

In my online teaching, I find that students are hesitant to question another student's postings on a discussion board or blog. Reluctance to question the ideas of others may be an outgrowth of a particular notion of manners, but it might cause unintended consequences. It is important to broach the topic of incorrect posts with your students early in the semester.

Within the larger concept of reconsidering the theoretical underpinnings of how they teach, professors must consider the ways in which students interact with content in an online course. Sims and Hedberg (2006) identify several types of interactive encounters—welcoming encounters, directing encounters, strategic encounters, ethical framing encounters, and personal narrative encounters—that students may have with other students, with the content, with the technology, and with the professor. Not all of these encounters are inherently present in all online classes; however, many or all of them may occur simultaneously in one course. Welcoming encounters typically involve students introducing themselves and learning to navigate the structure of the online learning environment. Directing encounters relate to the necessary structure and interaction in an online course. These encounters may or may not include the ability for learners and teachers to make choices about the learning. Strategic encounters relate to the ways in which learners' choices can lead to future learning. The more closely related the learner's interests are to the structure of the course, the more likely the learner is to be engaged with the content. Ethical framing encounters relate to the mores of the class; these may be similar to netiquette. They also include an understanding of policies related to plagiarism, using resources, and how students represent work as their own. Personal narrative encounters occur between students and the teacher and mainly function to personalize the experience of the online course. Sims and Hedberg state that narrative encounters relate to metacognition and can serve to build relationships. In their theoretical development of these different encounters, the authors theorize the underlying issues within these different scenarios. Within this framework of reconsidering theories of education, it is apparent that the social nature of learning is increasingly recognized as paramount for online learning.

Among the above encounters, it is ethical framing encounters that most closely relate to the scenario about students not questioning the posts of other students when they are wrong. As a faculty member who firmly believes in constructivism, I found this scenario quite a conundrum because the majority of questions that I pose or that other students pose are open-ended and allow for a variety of responses. However, I found that, at times, students misunderstood the question or the related readings and their posts were wrong. Because other students were hesitant to correct the incorrect posts, I needed to develop a strategy to handle this situation.

At the beginning of the semester, I now guide my students to an agreement about how and when the professor will step in to correct posts (Helms 2007). We discuss the following issues: How should corrections or revisions be made to posts—publicly by the professor to the discussion forum, privately by the professor to the one student only, or some combination of these? Could students act as monitors on a rotating basis to correct other student posts? How would this work? Could the professor notify students privately about an error in their post and then ask the students to correct it?

I found that it was essential to make this issue overt to the students at the beginning of the semester. Discussing the issue and giving students responsibility for monitoring discussion boards for the accuracy of information provided a shared sensibility about their learning. After trying this method, students were still hesitant to correct each other, but they were more willing to make posts to each other suggesting that their readings of the articles led them to different conclusions or that a classmate needed to go back and reread a certain section.

The question of incorrect posts raises an issue that I believe is unique to online environments, their asynchronicity. For example, a student may make an incorrect post at 12 noon on Monday; other students read it from 12:01 until 4:00 in the afternoon, when the professor makes an update or correction to the post, so students who read it after that point see the correct information. However, the students who already read it between 12:01 and 4:00 saw the incorrect information and may or may not revisit the post again. Though I continue to struggle with this issue and do not have good suggestions how to address it, other instructors who are contemplating teaching online should be aware of it.

Scenario: A student interprets another student's post as personally offensive and complains to the instructor about the message.

The first time this happened, I read the message deemed offensive by one student and simply could not see how it could possibly be interpreted as offensive. The post mentioned that some teachers were less than professional and were not consistently engaged with their job. The student who found it offensive was a teacher and I assumed that she took this as a personal attack, rather than a statement of another student's opinion. However, as I considered it later, I realized that a missing element online is the tone of voice, which significantly affects the meaning of a message. Thus, I now have an open discussion with students during the first week of an online class about tone of voice. We explore appropriate and inappropriate tones and how they can be manifested differently in an online environment as opposed to a classroom environment. I ask the students to discuss options for what they can do if they feel offended by what another student posted. Additionally, I tell students that if they have a concern about another student's tone or comments, they should address that concern directly with the specific student before coming to me. As a result of this early discussion, students seem better able to communicate with each other, ask others for clarification, or let a student know that a comment was offensive. Also, students are more careful in making their posts, often stating that they are playing devil's advocate or challenging someone's reasoning. Starting posts with a simple statement that it is intended as a test or challenge seems to defuse the potential offense that another student might infer from the post.

Scenario: Students make posts that contain, for example, racist, homophobic, xenophobic, or misogynistic words and concepts.

In the case described at the beginning of this chapter about the student making a blog post with offensive words, I chose to address this issue both publicly and privately. I made a post on the class blog to address it publicly, communicating to the entire class that what he posted was inappropriate and widely viewed as offensive. Then, I sent the student a private email in order to discuss how he had arrived at the ideas that he had posted. I learned that his ideas originated from a book published in the early 1960s related to the incorrect theory of eugenics. He came across this book while working on a college assignment in the early 1990s and was unaware of the offensive nature of the words he used. He and I engaged in a series of emails on this topic and exchanged many ideas about ways to discuss race with students at a variety of levels.

When I asked colleagues about this issue, they offered similar suggestions and also explored the importance of deleting inappropriate content as soon as possible and contacting the student individually to discuss the issue in depth (Stokrocki 2007). Another colleague mentioned the importance of the instructor being proactive and modeling good discussion. She also mentioned that she encourages students to work out issues among themselves. If this does not work, she asks students why they made the post that they did in order to remind all students of the need to challenge their assumptions (Lai 2007).

In the case that I opened the chapter with, I chose not to delete the comment because I wanted to address it publicly. If this one graduate student, a teacher in the public schools, was not aware of the offensive nature of the words that he used, I thought that others in the class might be unaware as well.

Summary

Meaningful discussions do not inherently happen in a face-to-face class and they also do not inherently happen in an online environment. Teachers and students need to recognize this and work collaboratively to build the positive environment necessary for an online course. In the humanities and the arts, instructors may have different concerns about teaching online as compared with other disciplines. Because of the subjective nature of some topics and the need for interpretation, discussions may have a wider range than those in science or math, for example. However, regardless of discipline, when teaching online it is important that faculty members reconsider theories of education and also build social interactions into their courses. To summarize my discussion in this chapter, I offer the following specific suggestions for building meaningful discussion:

- Create an ungraded social space on a discussion board or blog where students can interact in informal ways.
- Send the class periodic emails to promote thinking about the course, encourage students, and build interest in the course discussion.
- At the beginning of the course, lead a discussion about how incorrect posts will be handled and address how you will work together to correct these posts.
- Also at the beginning of the course, overtly address the issue of tone of voice and how students need to indicate their tone within their messages. This is especially important if students are playing devil's advocate or challenging another student's post.
- Find a way that you are comfortable with to address inappropriate content in students' posts. This may involve other students or you may choose to address the issue privately.

I hope that these suggestions, which arise from my own experiences and those of my colleagues, will help faculty members navigate the complex social issues that they may encounter when teaching online.

Notes

1. Though I recognize that many authors use different terms with subtle distinctions, I use the terms *online learning* and *distance learning* interchangeably. Waterhouse (2005) promotes the term *elearning*; however, because some of the instances that I discuss involve an online component of a face-to-face course, I choose not to use this term.

2. Because social interactions are so crucial to learning, I deliberately engaged with a number of colleagues, friends, and students to generate the ideas in this article. Special thanks to Kathryn R. Helms, Sara Wilson McKay, Mary Stockroki, and Alice Lai for their willingness to enter into this dialogue with me and explore these issues.

References

Burbules, Nicholas C. 2004. "Navigating the Advantages and Disadvantages of Online Pedagogy." In *Learning, Culture and Community in Online Education*, ed. Caroline Haythornthwaite and Michelle M. Kazmer, 3–17. New York: Peter Lang.

Dyke, Martin, Gráinne Conole, Andrew Ravenscroft, and Sara de Freitas. 2007. "Learning Theory and Its Application to E-learning." In *Contemporary Perspectives in E-learning Research: Themes, Methods and Impact on Practice*, ed. Gráinne Conole and Martin Oliver, 82–98. London: Routledge.

Edelstein, Susan, and Jason Edwards. 2002. "If You Build It, They Will Come: Building Learning Communities Through Threaded Discussions." *Online Journal of Distance Learning Administration* 5, no. 1. www.westga.edu/~distance/ojdla/spring51/edelstein51.html.

Haythornthwaite, Caroline, Michelle M. Kazmer, Jennifer Robbins, and Susan Shoemaker. 2004. "Community Development among Distance Learners: Temporal and Technological Dimensions." In *Learning, Culture and Community in Online Education*, ed. Caroline Haythornthwaite and Michelle M. Kazmer, 35–58. New York: Peter Lang.

Helms, Kathryn R. 2007. Personal communication, April 12.

Lai, Alice. 2007. Personal communication, December 20.

McKay, Sara Wilson. 2007. Personal communication, November 18.

Millan, Brett. 2009. *Value Differences Between Online Students and Face-to-Face Students at a College in South Texas*. PhD diss., Texas A&M University-Kingsville. *Dissertation Abstracts International*, Section A: Humanities and Social Sciences 69 (10-A): 3879.

Mishra, Sanjaya, and Charles Juwah. 2006. "Interactions in Online Discussions: A Pedagogical Perspective." In *Interactions in Online Education: Implications for Theory and Practice*, ed. Charles Juwah, 156–170. London: Routledge.

Orr, Robert, Mitchell R. Williams, and Kevin Pennington. 2009. "Institutional Efforts to Support Faculty in Online Teaching." *Innovations in Higher Education* 34: 257–268.

Palloff, Rena M., and Keith Pratt. 1999. *Building Learning Communities in Cyberspace*. San Francisco: Jossey-Bass.

―――. 2003. *The Virtual Student*. San Francisco: Jossey-Bass.

―――. 2007. *Building Online Learning Communities: Effective Strategies for the Virtual Classroom*. San Francisco: Jossey-Bass.

Paraskeva, Fotini, Sofia Mysirlaki, and Aikaterini Papagianni. 2010. "Multiplayer Online Games as Educational Tools: Facing New Challenges in Learning." *Computers and Education* 54: 498–505.

Pegrum, Mark. 2007. "Socrates and Plato Meet Neoliberalism in the Virtual Agora: Online Dialogue and the Development of Oppositional Pedagogies." In *Brave New Classrooms: Democratic Education and the Internet*, ed. Joe Lockard and Mark Pegrum, 13–34. New York: Peter Lang.

Simonson, Michael, Sharon Smaldino, Michael Albright, and Susan Zvacek. 2003. *Teaching and Learning at a Distance*. Upper Saddle River, NJ: Merrill Prentice Hall.

Sims, Rod, and John Hedberg. 2006. "Encounter Theory: A Model to Enhance Online Communication, Interaction, and Engagement." In *Interactions in Online Education: Implications for Theory and Practice*, ed. Charles Juwah, 27–45. London: Routledge.

Stokrocki, Mary. 2007. Personal communication, November 26.

Vygotsky, Lev S. 1978. *Mind in Society: The Development of Higher Psychological Processes*. Cambridge, MA: Harvard University Press.

Wagner, Mark. 2009. "Massively Multiplayer Online Role-Playing Games as Constructivist Learning Environments in K–12 Education: A Delphi Study." PhD diss., Waldon University. *Dissertation Abstracts International*, Section A: Humanities and Social Sciences 69 (8-A): 3124.

Waterhouse, Shirley. 2005. *The Power of eLearning: The Essential Guide for Teaching in the Digital Age*. Boston: Pearson.

9

Easier Than It Looks

Using Web Resources in the Humanities

Daryl E. Fridley

The Internet is an incredible tool for teachers in the humanities. A vast virtual repository containing the creative efforts of millions of people working over thousands of years in various media, the web holds great potential for an instructor attempting to guide students through a study of the human condition. Although many of the resources found on the web have long been available in university libraries, luring students into those buildings is frequently a challenge. In the context of this essay, I will skirt the question of whether or not students *should* go to the library and simply assert that, if they do not cross the library threshold, they will not be able to use the resources that you want them to use. If the resources are on the web, though, the situation is different.

While it is unlikely that, should you drop by the library in the next few minutes, you would find several of your students mingling near the existential philosophy or medieval French literature section, many of them probably are—at this very moment—in virtual proximity to similar kinds of resources. In fact, they probably spend several hours a day just a click of the mouse away from items not much different from those available in a brick-and-mortar library. A few years ago, a study commissioned by Yahoo! (Harris 2003) found that young people from twelve to twenty-four spent more time on the web (16.7 hours per week) than with any other media, including television (13.6 hours), cell phones (7.7 hours), and printed literature not related to schoolwork (6 hours). Since the study was published, the expansion of sites such as iTunes, Facebook, and YouTube, as well as expanded access to online content through mobile devices, has increased the reasons for young people to get online. This "wired generation" has grown up interacting with the various types of media available online. Prensky (2001) describes them as "digital natives" and refers to those who predate them on the evolutionary timeline of technology as "digital immigrants." Assigning students to use web-based resources allows them to continue working in an environment with which they are already familiar, increasing the possibility that they will engage more fully in the study of your discipline.

Before you can begin sending students out on the web, however, you need to know *where* to send them. In order to effectively exploit the fact that they are already hanging out in the "library," you need to have some sense of how to find and use relevant resources on the web.

Types of Resources

That the web, with its impressive collections of historical documents, philosophical treatises, representations of visual art, musical performances, poems, short stories, and even novels, might be useful to teachers seems obvious. Knowing how to begin finding and using the resources relevant to a particular course may seem a more complicated matter, but it is not. In fact, you can find and use web resources in much the same manner that you have traditionally found and used resources for your courses. These resources can, generally, be divided into two broad groups: primary observations and reflections and secondary interpretations of those observations and reflections. Both types of resources can be found in abundance on the web.

Since "showing" is almost always more effective than "telling," showing you the ease with which the web might be mined for course resources is the point of this essay. Such a demonstration is undermined, however, by the fact that what I want to show you is on the web . . . and this chapter is not. To remedy this weakness, I have included in the text the address of each website noted as an example, in addition to listing them at the end of the chapter. My hope is that you will take the time to explore many of these sites as you read, allowing your own curiosity to guide you toward a greater familiarity with humanities resources on the web. Since I teach history, most of my examples relate most directly to that discipline, but many of the websites mentioned include resources relevant to other areas of the humanities. It will certainly take more time to reach the last paragraph of the chapter if you read in this interactive manner, but, by the time you do, you will have not only read *about* resources available on the web, but also spent a fair amount of time actually exploring them.

Primary Observations and Reflections

In the humanities, scholars and students are interested in people, and so the primary data consist of the observations and reflections recorded by other human beings. Each area of the humanities specializes in using particular kinds of raw materials to construct meaningful insight into the human condition. In the same way that carpenters work with wood, for example, historians work with letters, journals, maps, and other primary sources. Although various fields focus on different subjects or types of materials, at the core of every discipline included in the humanities are artifacts documenting what other people have seen, heard, felt, believed, and observed. Instructors often integrate examples of these primary resources into their courses so that students can analyze how professionals in the discipline arrive at particular conclusions and so that they can learn to evaluate similar information according to the standards of the discipline. In my field, history, we sometimes refer to this process as learning to "think historically." Traditionally, instructors required a student to buy a collection of primary sources, made copies of sources from their own collections, or sent the student to the library to find primary sources housed there. The web offers greater accessibility to a larger number, and more varied types, of these resources.

For example, links to hundreds of primary sources may be found at the Internet History Sourcebooks Project (www.fordham.edu/halsall). The Sourcebooks are organized by both chronology (e.g., ancient, medieval, and modern) and subject (e.g., African, Islamic, women), making it relatively easy to find an example of the twelfth-century Islamic poet Omar Khayyam's work (www.fordham.edu/halsall/source/omarkhayyam-wisdom.html) or a copy of *Beowulf* in Old English (www.fordham.edu/halsall/basis/beowulf-oe.html). While some links will connect you to pages within the Sourcebooks site, others will take you to pages housed elsewhere on the web, where you will often find even more primary sources. The Sourcebooks Project is housed on the Fordham University website, and other educational institutions across the globe have also invested in making primary sources available. Through its various digital collections (www.odl.ox.ac.uk/collections/index.html), Oxford University, for example, provides access to an array of documents, works of art, and images of artifacts—from medieval manuscripts (www.bodley.ox.ac.uk/dept/scwmss/wmss/medieval) to sixteenth-century broadside ballads (www.bodley.ox.ac.uk/ballads/ballads.htm).

As you are no doubt aware, governments—bureaucratic behemoths that they are—keep many records. In recent years, governmental entities have begun to make many of these records available to the public through the Internet. The American Memory collection of the Library of Congress (http://memory.loc.gov/ammem/index.html) is particularly valuable. Of course, the collection is largely limited to topics related to the United States, but within those parameters, the resources available are extensive. The site is easily searchable by subject and format and includes a variety of media types, allowing students, for example, to listen to southern folk music recorded in the 1930s (http://memory.loc.gov/ammem/lohtml/lohome.html), to watch early film footage of Teddy Roosevelt (http://memory.loc.gov/ammem/collections/troosevelt_film/index.html), or to analyze nineteenth-century photographs of Native American women (http://photoswest.org/exhib/gallery4/leadin.htm). The National Archives (www.archives.gov) is another governmental institution that has expended a great deal of effort to make historical documents accessible, offering a collection that includes much more than the founding documents you might expect. Other nations, such as Japan (www.archives.go.jp/english/index.html), the United Kingdom (www.nationalarchives.gov.uk), and Egypt (www.nationalarchives.gov.eg/nae/home.jsp), also have archives that function similarly.

In addition to these traditional institutional collections, you can also find useful materials at some more unconventional websites. One of these is the Internet Archive (www.archive.org/index.php), a burgeoning online library. While the site does contain text resources, its unique value lies in its "Moving Images" collection, which includes over 500 hours of speeches made by President George W. Bush (www.archive.org/details/george_bush_archive), global television coverage of the September 11, 2001 attacks (www.archive.org/details/sept_11_tv_archive), and Universal Newsreels from 1929 to 1967 (www.archive.org/details/universal_newsreels). Even more unconventional is the dynamic, user-driven video repository YouTube (www.youtube.com). Because uploads to YouTube are not regulated by any sort of academic standards, the site must be used with special care, but the resources available on the site warrant the effort required by extra scrutiny. Items in YouTube's "collection" change frequently, so I will not cite specific web addresses here, but, if you want to use Lyndon Johnson's 1964 "Daisy" ad or James Brown singing "I'm Black and I'm Proud" or a clip of Leonard Bernstein discussing Beethoven, you can find it by searching YouTube.

Directing students to a particular resource, however, does not guarantee that they will know how to use it. People are not born knowing how to make sense of primary observations and reflections, so learning to analyze and interpret historical documents, orchestral compositions, literary texts, or philosophical treatises is also an important part of a humanities course. This process includes examining the context in which the primary resource was created and applying the standards of a particular discipline to its interpretation. While you provide the principal instruction regarding how to interpret and use such materials, additional resources that support and expand your instruction are also available on the web. The American Social History Project's History Matters site (http://historymatters.gmu.edu) is one example. In addition to having over 1,000 primary source documents, reviewed and annotated by professional historians, the site includes an entire section focused on how to use different kinds of primary sources (http://historymatters.gmu.edu/browse/makesense). Here, students can read about the particular idiosyncrasies of working with oral histories, old maps, and other types of resources. Taking this how-to process a step further is a collaborative project sponsored by the Center for History and New Media and the Stanford University School of Education. At Historical Thinking Matters (http://historicalthinkingmatters.org), students can work through the steps of analyzing a historical document, with professional suggestions and responses readily available. Based largely on the work of codirector Sam Wineburg's research (2001) on how people learn to think historically, these interactive exercises introduce students to the types of questions historians might ask when studying documents related to the Spanish-American War, the Scopes trial, the inception of Social Security, and the refusal of Rosa Parks to give up her seat on the bus.

Expert scholarly guidance, in conjunction with meaningful practice, is essential to students' development of disciplinary skills and knowledge. Important, too, are examples of the work done by scholars in the humanities as they struggle to interpret primary observations and reflections.

Secondary Interpretations

When you assign excerpts from monographs or have students read journal articles, you are exposing them to models of disciplinary work. To be sure, you usually want them to remember the conclusions drawn by these authors, but also you want them to observe how the scholars in question arrived at those conclusions and how they used certain kinds of data to justify their interpretations. These two formats have long dominated classrooms because of their convenience and the fact that they represent the ways in which scholars have most frequently presented their findings, and those two traits continue to commend them even in this new digital age. To these traditional examples of scholarly work, the web generally adds little. Most monographs are still published on paper, and many academic journals, though available online through university library portals, have restricted access.

While many academics continue to share their findings via the written word, others prefer to present their conclusions in multimedia exhibits. This is, of course, not a new development. Public scholars have long presented their conclusions in museum exhibits. Access, however, has often been fairly restricted: field trips to the National Museum of American History or the Louvre are not practical for students in most college courses. The advent of the web has created new possibilities by making virtual field trips to these (http://americanhistory.si.edu/index.cfm; www.louvre.fr/llv/commun/home.jsp?bmLocale=en) and other world museums practical. Most museums have already moved to exploit these new possibilities.

Online exhibits can be powerful, in part, because their curators can include source materials that must be left out of written interpretations, either because of technical reasons (e.g., audio or video clips) or space limitations. For example, an exhibition on the rescue of Danish Jews in 1943 (www.ushmm.org/museum/exhibit/focus/danish) at the United States Holocaust Memorial Museum (www.ushmm.org) benefits measurably from the inclusion of a video interview with one of the participants. Similarly, a web presentation on the abolition of slavery at American Memory (www.loc.gov/exhibits/african/afam005.html) integrates narrative with abolitionist handbills, songs, and newspapers. When these types of source materials are included in exhibits, the process by which scholars arrive at their conclusion is made more transparent. Online exhibits, then, frequently function both as examples of scholarly work and as repositories of primary resources.

One of the concerns about using historical products found on the web is that nearly anybody with a computer, decent software, and Internet access can create an online exhibit that appears reliable, especially to the untrained eyes of students. There is a degree of security that goes with knowing that an article or book had to go through the editing process. A similar degree of security surrounds exhibits hosted by credible institutions such as the Schomburg Center for Research in Black Culture (www.nypl.org/research/sc/sc.html), the Museum of Modern Art (www.moma.org), or St. Petersburg's State Hermitage Museum (www. hermitagemuseum.org/html_En/index.html). It is worth remembering, however, that the validity of an interpretation lies in the application of disciplinary standards and not with an institutional association. As students struggle to construct their own conclusions, exposure to noninstitutional exhibits might help them realize that intelligent interpretation is not the exclusive domain of professional academics. One example is Mūsarium (www.musarium.com), a collection of audiovisual compilations with topics ranging from U.S. involvement in Vietnam (www.musarium.com/stories/vietnaminc/index.html) to lynching in the early twentieth century (www.withoutsanctuary.org). Although such nonacademic websites may require you to exercise a greater degree of scholarly judgment, the web can open your students to the ways in which people use your discipline outside of the academy.

Clearly, the kinds of resources available on the Internet are not too different from the resources you are already using in your courses. The web offers access to a greater number and variety of these primary and secondary resources, but it does not actually require you to teach much differently than you have in the past. Using the web merely expands your repertoire . . . but only if you can find materials relevant to your courses.

Locating Materials

Despite my attempt to use examples that would apply to a wide variety of teachers, it is unlikely that I have provided you with an extensive list of web resources that meets your specific needs. The practical challenge of locating resources appropriate for your particular courses remains. In theory, the Internet is an endless gold mine of teaching treasures, a pedagogical paradise. The web's theoretically infinite potential is of little practical value, however, if you do not know how to find, in the midst of billions of websites, resources that will enable you to effectively engage students in a meaningful study of your discipline.

In order to address this issue, it is useful to once again return to the analogy of the web as a kind of library. If you were to walk into a large university library with absolutely no notion of how the holdings were arranged or catalogued, you would be overwhelmed. With millions of items in various media on several floors, the chances of finding something that you could use in a course would be ridiculously low. Luckily, when you walk into your institution's library, you have a sense of how it is organized and how to find items that might be useful to you. There are, generally speaking, two ways in which you locate items in a library, and both of those methods work on the web also: searching for specific items and browsing the field.

Searching

The first method is to query the library's electronic catalog. If you want to find a copy of *Art as Experience* by John Dewey in your university library, you type in that title and the catalog provides you with information about the book's availability and location. In a similar manner, you can locate specific resources on the web using search engines like Google (www.google.com) or Yahoo! (http://search.yahoo.com). Once you decide, for example, that you would like your students to study a draft of Lincoln's Gettysburg Address (www.loc.gov/exhibits/gadd/images/frstdrt1.jpg) or view a copy of Picasso's *Guernica* (www.artchive.com/artchive/p/picasso/guernica.jpg), a quick search will provide you with links to those items.

Sometimes, however, you do not have a specific item in mind when you enter the library but, instead, have only a general notion of what you want. You might be interested, for example, in assigning your world lit class a novel by Carlos Fuentes but have not decided on a specific title. Sitting down at one of the library computers, you type in "Fuentes, Carlos," and the locations of all the library's materials related to Carlos Fuentes are immediately displayed on the screen. Similarly, a web search can be helpful even when you do not have a specific item in mind. Searching for "Mark Twain writings" returns a list of sites that include both information about the author and copies of many of his books and essays. Similarly, a search for "primary sources U.S. Civil War" identifies several locations where you can find firsthand accounts and reflections on the conflict.

The likelihood of a successful search is influenced, in part, by the ability to imagine the existence of a particular resource or type of resource. If it does not occur to you that a recording of Winston Churchill's "never surrender" speech might be useful in your class's study of World War II Britain or that it might be available to you (www.signalalpha.com/World_War_Two.html), then you might never think to search for it. While you would probably have little trouble imagining that you could find a copy of the Declaration of Independence (www.archives.gov/exhibits/charters/declaration.html) or a picture of Frank Lloyd Wright's Fallingwater (www.paconserve.org/index-fw1.asp) on the web, you might be less likely to imagine the existence of less traditional kinds of resources, such as audio recordings, video recordings, and online exhibits. Once you realize, however, that items like recordings of former slaves describing their experiences in bondage (http://memory.loc.gov/ammem/collections/voices/index.html) or the Smithsonian's interactive exhibit on the artist Edward Hopper (http://americanart.si.edu/exhibitions/online/hopper) exist on the web, your imagination will expand to incorporate a plethora of new possibilities.

Undoubtedly, you began this essay in hopes that it might include suggestions less obvious than "Google it." Sometimes, though, the simplest approach is the one most easily overlooked. Using the web as a source for teaching tools is no more difficult or exotic than using it to find election returns, baseball scores, or tomorrow's weather. In fact, you have probably already thought of some specific resources for which you would like to search. Maybe you have an old, dog-eared copy of an essay that you have used for years in your class, and you are wondering if you could find a replacement copy of it on the web. Or maybe you have searched your institution's library for a firsthand account of a particular historical event but had little luck finding something that you think would be accessible to your students. Or perhaps you have taught a face-to-face course for some time, but next semester will be teaching it online. You may have all the necessary resources safely stored in a file folder in your desk, but finding copies of them on the web would be much easier than having to scan and upload each one to the course website. The simple act of reviewing your course syllabus will likely provide you with several "I wonder if *that* is on the web" moments. In fact, it might be a good idea to search for some of these items while they are still fresh in your mind. You may be surprised at how many of them you find on the web. It is the search itself, though, that will likely open you to the true possibilities of the Internet.

Browsing

If you did indeed pause in your reading to spend some time searching for specific electronic resources, you probably also engaged in the second way of locating interesting and useful items in the library: browsing. You might enter the library looking for a specific text on the history of Chinese block printing and find it on a shelf next to dozens of other works on Chinese art. Many of these may be books you never knew existed, on related topics that had not occurred to you. You begin to browse, and before you know it, you have spent an hour exploring nearby shelves. Only planning to quickly pick up one book, you end up leaving the library with five or six.

Browsing the web can work in a similar fashion—as you probably found out if you paused above to search for specific items. Perhaps you teach a course on Eastern religions and want to find out if there is a copy of the *Bhagavad-Gita* on the web. Searching for that text, you find it available at several sites. Scrolling through the results, you choose the location www.sacred-texts.com/hin/gita/. A translation of the sacred Hindu text can indeed be found here, but at the top of the page are two additional hyperlinks. The one on the left reads "Sacred Texts" and the other "Hinduism." Clicking on the right link takes you to a page containing hyperlinks to several other Hindu texts that might prove useful in your course. The left link opens up an even broader opportunity for exploration: electronic paths to hundreds of the world's sacred texts.

This type of browsing is one of the most effective ways to discover resources on the web that you might use in your classes. It allows your own interests—defined by the initial search—to direct you to the types of webpages on which you might find useful items. Just like my earlier suggestion that you search for items useful to your course, the idea that you might simply browse the web is not particularly novel. Assuming that you began this essay with some degree of online experience, it is likely that you spend some time every week exploring areas of interest on the web in this fashion. In fact, many sites are designed specifically to encourage this type of behavior. If, for example, you go to the page on which Amazon.com offers Rousseau's *The Social Contract* for sale, you will find links to other books by Rousseau and to books bought by other shoppers who also bought *The Social Contract and Discourses*. Inherent in the design of many websites, commercial or not, is the notion that "if you are interested in the current page, then you may be interested in *this* one." This inclination of web designers to link their sites to related ones makes the web an optimal browsing environment. Given that your own experiences have probably already borne out this fact, I reiterate it here only to make the point, once again, that finding web resources is not nearly as complex or daunting as some may believe it to be.

Conclusion

The Internet contains more resources than you or I could ever use and places those items in an environment in which many students already spend much of their time. At first glance, however, the notion of choosing specific, useful resources out of the billions of choices available may seem overwhelmingly difficult. It is not. To be sure, it is possible to use the web in more complex and nuanced ways that rely on evolving technologies, but those are probably not the best place to start. Instead, by simply drawing upon the skills you have developed as a teacher and your extensive knowledge of your discipline, you can begin to use the web in a fashion similar to how you have used traditional libraries. Despite the size and complexity of the web itself, mining it for course materials is easier than it looks.

References

Harris Interactive and Teenage Research Unlimited. 2003. *Born to Be Wired: The Role of New Media for a Digital Generation*. Sunnyvale, CA: Yahoo! and Carat Interactive.

Prensky, Marc. 2001. "Digital Natives, Digital Immigrants." *On the Horizon* 9, no. 5: 1–6.

Wineburg, Sam. 2001. *Historical Thinking and Other Unnatural Acts: Charting the Future of Teaching the Past*. Philadelphia: Temple University Press.

Websites Cited

"The African-American Mosaic." 2005. Library of Congress. www.loc.gov/exhibits/african/afam005.html.

Allen, J., and J. Littlefield. 2005. "Without Sanctuary." Mūsarium. www.without-sanctuary.org.

The American Folklife Center. 2007. "Southern Mosaic: The John and Ruby Lomax 1939 Southern States Recording Trip." Library of Congress. http://memory.loc.gov/ammem/lohtml/lohome.html.

"American Memory." n.d. Library of Congress. http://memory.loc.gov/ammem/index.html.

American Social History Project. 2005. "History Matters." Center for Media and Learning and the Center for History and New Media. http://historymatters.gmu.edu.

———. 2005. "Making Sense of Evidence." Center for Media and Learning and the Center for History and New Media. http://historymatters.gmu.edu/browse/makesense.

"The Bhagavad Gita." n.d. Internet Sacred Text Archive. www.sacred-texts.com/hin/gita.

"Declaration of Independence." n.d. National Archives of the United States. www.archives.gov/exhibits/charters/declaration.html.

"An Edward Hopper Scrapbook." 1999. Smithsonian American Art Museum. http://americanart.si.edu/exhibitions/online/hopper.

"Fallingwater." 2008. Western Pennsylvania Conservancy. www.paconserve.org/index-fw1.asp.

"George W. Bush Presidential Speech Archive." n.d. Internet Archive. www.archive.org/details/george_bush_archive.

"Gettysburg Address." n.d. Library of Congress. www.loc.gov/exhibits/gadd/images/frstdrt1.jpg.

"Google." 2010. Google. www.google.com.

Griffiths, Philip Jones. 2002. "Vietnam Inc." Mūsarium. www.musarium.com/stories/vietnaminc/index.html.

"Guernica." n.d. Artchive. www.artchive.com/artchive/p/picasso/guernica.jpg.

Halsall, Paul, ed. 1996. "The Internet History Sourcebooks Project." Internet History Sourcebooks Project. www.fordham.edu/halsall.

———. 1998. "Beowulf (in Old English)." Internet History Sourcebooks Project. www.fordham.edu/halsall/basis/beowulf-oe.html.

———. 1998. "Omar Khayyam: The Wisdom of the Supreme, c. 1120." Internet History Sourcebooks Project. www.fordham.edu/halsall/source/omarkhayyam-wisdom.html.

"Historical Thinking Matters." n.d. Center of History and New Media and the Stanford University School of Education. http://historicalthinkingmatters.org.

"The Internet Archive." 1996. The Internet Archive. www.archive.org/index.php.

"MoMA." 2009. Museum of Modern Art. www.moma.org.

"Mūsarium." 2003. Musarium. www.musarium.com.

"Musée du Louvre." 2010. Musée du Louvre. www.louvre.fr/llv/commun/home.jsp?bmLocale=en.

"The National Archives." n.d. National Archives of the United Kingdom. www.nationalarchives.gov.uk.

"The National Archives." n.d. National Archives of the United States. www.archives.gov.

"The National Archives of Egypt." n.d. National Archives of Egypt. www.nationalarchives.gov.eg/nae/home.jsp.

"National Archives of Japan." 2007. National Archives of Japan. www.archives.go.jp/english/index.html.

"The National Museum of American History." n.d. Smithsonian Institution. http://americanhistory.si.edu/index.cfm.

"Native American Women." Denver Public Library. http://photoswest.org/exhib/gallery4/leadin.htm.

Oxford Digital Library. 1999. "The *Allegro* Catalog of Ballads." Bodleian Library, Oxford University. www.bodley.ox.ac.uk/ballads/ballads.htm.

———. 1999. "Western Manuscripts to *c.* 1500." Bodleian Library, Oxford University. www.bodley.ox.ac.uk/dept/scwmss/wmss/medieval.

———. 2003. "Digital Collections at Oxford University." Oxford University Library Services. www.odl.ox.ac.uk/collections/index.html.

"The Rescue of the Jews of Denmark." n.d. United States Holocaust Memorial Museum. www.ushmm.org/museum/exhibit/focus/danish.

"Schomburg Center for Research in Black Culture." 2009. New York Public Library. www.nypl.org/research/sc/sc.html.

"September 11 Television Archive." n.d. Internet Archive. www.archive.org/details/sept_11_tv_archive.

"The State Hermitage Museum." 2006. State Hermitage Museum, St. Petersburg. www.hermitagemuseum.org/html_En/index.html.

"Theodore Roosevelt: His Life and Times on Film." n.d. Library of Congress. http://memory.loc.gov/ammem/collections/troosevelt_film/index.html.

"The United States Holocaust Memorial Museum." n.d. United States Holocaust Memorial Museum. www.ushmm.org.

"Universal News Reels." n.d. Internet Archive. www.archive.org/details/universal_newsreels.

"Voices From the Days of Slavery." n.d. Library of Congress. http://memory.loc.gov/ammem/collections/voices/index.html.

"World War II History and Speeches." n.d. Signal Alpha. www.signalalpha.com/World_War_Two.html.

"Yahoo!" 2009. Yahoo. http://search.yahoo.com.

"YouTube." 2009. YouTube, LLC. www.youtube.com.

10

Assessing Student Learning Online

Martha Henckell

The lesson plan has been completed, the lectures and presentations created, the course activities and assignments developed, the course management system set up, and all required files uploaded to the server. *The End* . . . right? While some educators may take a backseat at this time and simply monitor the progress of assignment completion, it is actually the moment to gear up and assess whether learning actually occurs. Evidence of the work involved in the development of courses belies the idea that a diligent educator would consciously leave student learning to chance. But if learning is not assessed through the progress of the course, that is exactly what happens. Any course improvement would occur inadvertently.

In this chapter, my objective is to provide guidelines and techniques that can be used when assessing student learning online for the purpose of continuous course improvement. I use the terms *assessment* and *evaluation* interchangeably, with the focus on discovering whether student learning is occurring and at what level. Definitions and descriptions are provided as to what constitutes learning, how assessment leads to more effective teaching, what I do to evaluate learning, and the different types and purposes of assessment. Seven assessment procedures demonstrate the sequential steps involved in performing an assessment. Closure on the topic culminates with examples of techniques that can be used to assess learning.

What Constitutes Learning?

Learning is not a by-product; it is the principal product of teaching. Educators recognize this fact but one has to wonder if students sometimes hold a different mind-set. During my fourteen years in higher education, I have often been asked by students "Did I pass?" but never have I been asked, "Did I learn?" Christopher, Thomas, and Tallent-Runnels (2004) define learning as the development of relationships between the data provided that actually produces change. While students understand the meaning of grades, they may experience more difficulty defining or even recognizing that learning occurred. It is the educator's job not only to understand how students learn (Hutchinson 2007), but also to assist them in their journey of learning how to learn (Judith Mousley, as cited by Hutchinson).

Learning can be affected by many forces. Increasing course-related knowledge and skills can be influenced by the student's prior knowledge and creative, critical, and problem-solving skills (Christopher, Tallent-Runnels, and Thomas 2004; Palmer, Holt, and Bray 2008; Price and Randall 2008). Reaction to instructional methods also plays a role in the learning process (Gaytan and McEwen 2007). This includes students' reactions to teachers and teaching, class activities, assignments, and materials. In addition, students' attitudes and values can reduce the effectiveness of a course (Asselin 2003). To maximize the learning potential, all the factors that affect student learning should be assessed by both the instructor and the student.

I get to know my students' interests, values, current knowledge, and strengths and weaknesses by asking pointed questions in a forum. In addition, I ask my students to complete a free learning survey that I located on the Internet. Once they have saved the learning survey, I direct them to place the file in my dropbox so I, too, will be aware of their learning styles. Not relying solely on information gained from self-reported answers, I also monitor all student-instructor and student-student interactions for clues.

Education is about making connections. Students must recognize the benefit of the knowledge being imparted and make connections between the course objectives and assignments. For genuine learning to occur, students must use the new information and skills provided to make new connections that will then lead to changes in their environment (Christopher, Tallent-Runnels, and Thomas 2004). Instructors must also make connections; most importantly, they need to determine whether or not learning ensued. Assignments and activities completed by online students can provide the best evidence that connections were made and the goal of learning was realized. In a distance-learning environment, these connections will often occur as a result of tasks that involve online communications between students and other students, faculty, and university service and support providers such as the bookstore, information technology, and the library (Illinois Online Network 2010). Besides checking for knowledge gained, I also seek to understand students' attitudes and values in my review of these interactions.

The most important knowledge to be acquired in a course should be explicitly identified and communicated to online students. Connections between students and the major course concepts can thus be made and relationships developed more effortlessly, consequently building an expressway to a higher level of learning (Fink 2003). I approach this task by sharing a map that I build for myself when I develop a course. For example, when I create an assignment for a unit, I critically review the assignment to identify its purpose, or what the student will gain by completing it, and how the activities will meet that purpose. In an online course, the learning environment is largely student-centered. As a result of taking the guesswork out of the learning process, students should have a pleasurable learning experience. They will not have to question why or where, in the mountain of information being thrust upon them, the majority of their time and energy should be allotted.

As learning transpires, it can progress to any one of the six levels of cognitive skills: knowledge, comprehension, application, analysis, synthesis, and evaluation (Bloom 1956). Bloom's concept was enlarged upon by Anderson and Krathwohl (2001; Christopher, Tallent-Runnels, and Thomas 2004) to include four types of knowledge: factual, conceptual, procedural, and metacognitive. The extent to which knowledge is augmented will rely on the efforts of both the educator and student. Before diving in to assess your class, however, there is more to learn.

What Is Assessment?

Once the course is launched, the management phase begins: time for the educator to begin directing and controlling the learning process. This cannot be accomplished without assessing the progress of knowledge, understanding, abilities, or skills acquired by the students in relation to the course's learning objectives established by the educator (QAA 2006), and assessment cannot be accurately accomplished unless actual data are collected. Asselin (2003) encourages the use of multiple types of data and adds to the list above a need to assess strategies used and attitude present. Only by monitoring and measuring student development can I provide appropriate feedback and support and then make the necessary course alterations to ensure that my instruction has been effective.

Assessment of learning is a win-win situation. I win because I discover the many learning styles exhibited by my students. Armed with information about the learners' learning traits, whether positioned between holistic and analytic, verbal and spatial, reflective and impulsive, or exploratory and passive, I can modify my course to better meet their needs before the course ends. If assessment is conducted properly, students win because they will become aware of what they do and do not understand, thus becoming more engaged and more motivated to participate in the learning process (Marriott 2009). Without timely and pertinent feedback from the performance of valid assessments, students may proceed through the online coursework uninvolved, unmotivated, and unaware of misconceptions until the opportunity to increase knowledge is gone.

Effective teaching goes hand-in-hand with assessment. If my goal is to be an effective teacher, I must continually assess my virtual classroom. Various assessment techniques allow me to discern not only if the students are learning, but also how they learn in response to the instructional methods used (Angelo and Cross 1993). Using valid assessment instruments, I will be able to objectively measure the level of learning present for each individual. If the correct assessment type is chosen and correctly applied, both students and the instructor will reap the benefits.

Types of Assessment

The desired outcome of any project is more likely to be achieved if the end result is identified before undertaking the project. The same holds true when developing an assessment plan. Checking for understanding can be accomplished with both formative and summative assessments (Colburn 2009; Fairfield-Sonn et al. 2009). As if the whole assessment process is not confusing enough, conflicting definitions of the two types are prolifically spread throughout the literature. To separate the meanings of the two, I consider formative assessments as first-level assessments. Formative assessments take place "just in time," when it is not too late for teachers to revise their instructional methods in order to provide an opportunity for current students to improve or increase learning. Points for grading purposes may or may not be assigned when performing a formative assessment. Summative assessments, on the other hand, provide a summation of the event that just occurred—that is, an exam following the end of an instructional unit—and primarily result in an appointment of grades.

The type of evaluation tool used can provide either a direct or indirect assessment. The key to choosing the correct assessment technique is to understand the purpose of the assessment. With the direct method, what has been learned is compared to measurable learning outcomes (Rogers 2006). Assignments that allow for a performance appraisal—that is, exams, reports, and other projects—are used to directly assess learning. While this method is considered stronger and is more frequently used, not all learning activity can be discerned using a direct approach; that is when the use of an indirect approach is appropriate. If I seek to identify a change in my students' attitudes, values, or perceptions, I would use indirect assessment tools such as student interviews or surveys. Whether the direct or indirect method is chosen, all assessments have their limitations and bias.

Assessment Procedures

Basically there are seven steps to follow when performing an assessment, regardless of the learning environment. Wells (2006) identifies the procedures related to the task of conducting assessments as (1) develop the assessment, (2) distribute the associated student assignment, (3) administer the assessment, (4) collect and store submissions, (5) evaluate submissions, (6) record comments and scores or grade, and (7) deliver feedback and results to students. Guidelines regarding each of these procedures follow.

Develop the Assessment

In a traditional classroom, faculty members often use an informal method of assessment. They make judgments based on students' facial expressions, body language, questions, and comments. Unfortunately, when this informal method is used, the messages students send can be misleading or incorrect. An advantage that I have found in teaching a well-constructed online course compared to a traditional course is that it is more difficult for students to conceal their lack of understanding until exam time rolls around. Basic foundational knowledge is easily gleaned from the activities that are required when teaching in a virtual environment (Magnussen 2008). When teaching online, I have discovered that

I can best assess learning by performing a course-embedded assessment. This procedure requires the evaluation of student work products that are aligned with established course objectives (Gerretson and Golson 2005). These products may result from brief assignments, requiring the students to produce only a few lines of comment in response to a question I pose about a semester-long project, such as a journal that I can review throughout the course.

Once the criteria instrument has been developed, it should be shared with students when the task is assigned (Lei 2008). For an assessment to provide accurate information, my students must be aware of the level of knowledge that I am seeking. By clearly identifying and communicating my assessment criteria, I am setting students up for success. I am also saving myself time that would be wasted by attempting to improve my instruction when the students actually knew more than they communicated in the assignments.

Distribute the Associated Student Assignment

One of the most frequently used assessment assignments is objective tests that require little or no written feedback from instructors and online students. Types of common objective tests include multiple-choice, true-or-false, matching, and fill-in-the-blank. When creating assignments for assessment purposes, I avoid relying only on the use of objective tests unless my goal is to measure a relatively low-level cognitive function of recalling facts.

Online assignments that can be used to assess learning include research reports, projects, visual presentations, discussion boards, case studies, forums, and journals. Gaytan and McEwen (2007) recommend that major assignments such as these have an associated grading rubric developed and delivered with the task. I frequently use briefer and quicker assignments to evaluate learning as well. My philosophy is not to wait until students have completed end-of-unit activities before assessing their level of understanding.

Administer the Assessment

In a study conducted by Gaytan and McEwen (2007), instructors ranked the most effective methods for assessing assignments as rubrics, peer evaluation, and self-assessment. Students ranked the most effective methods as self-assessments, weekly assignments with immediate feedback, and use of rubrics. As a faculty member, I may use one method or a combination. My choice will depend on factors such as what method will provide the most benefit to the students and the amount of time available to perform assessor tasks that will allow time for the results to be used.

Collect and Store Submissions

In an online class, this step is made simple because I require all student products to be created in a digital format and either sent to me as an email attachment or placed in a purchased or homegrown learning management system. After the course ends, I can permanently save the submissions on my computer, where they can be accessed at any time.

Evaluate Submissions

Prior to the submission of student products for evaluation, the instructor should already have decided whether a score or grade will be assigned. Whether recorded or not, I find a score helpful in quickly quantifying the level of learning. Numbers allow me to calculate averages, highs, and lows. By using scores, I also enable students to quickly judge how much they do or do not know. In light of the fact that some of my students are not motivated to perform their best or even complete the assigned work without an associated grade, I generally consign points. The more intense the assignment is, the higher I place the grade value.

A major challenge of assessment is fairly evaluating the learning of students with poor writing skills. When an instructor assesses the students' achievement of course objectives and also the quality of their writing, an inconsistency and inequality in evaluating student learning may result (Liang and Creasy 2004). My motto is to assess only what I list in the criteria that I previously provided to my students. If writing with a particular skill set is listed as an intended goal, then the students should expect to lose points for poor writing. But if my recorded purpose for assessment is to check students' understanding of how the culture of a community changes following a disaster, then the completeness of the response is the criterion I apply when assigning a score or grade.

In order to ensure consistency, Gerretson and Golson (2005) recommend using the same outcomes and rubrics when assessing learning in multiple sections of the same course. Educators must indeed avoid taking a subjective view that could result in unreliable, inconsistent, and unequal scoring and evaluation of student learning (Liang and Creasy 2004). In my courses, I most often use rubrics to guard against making judgments; by doing so, I adhere to what the data reveal.

Of course, in the process of performing an assessment of learning, instructors must examine content for evidence of cheating or plagiarism, otherwise, they cannot properly assess what that particular student or group of students have learned. Free software applications are available to help faculty quickly and easily determine whether students are plagiarizing. By conducting a search on the key words "checking for plagiarism," the instructor can get the results of multiple free software options that allow entire documents, not just suspicious phrases, to be loaded and checked.

Record Comments and Scores or Grade

If I assigned points to the criteria listed in my assessment, it would be during the sixth step that I record the performance grades. On certain assignments, my comments or feedback on the activity will be directed at and for the benefit of the group as a whole. At other times, my comments are directed at students individually and in private, where only the individual can access them. When evaluating an activity created in Microsoft Word, I can easily track changes that resulted from my feedback comments included in a draft document. Regardless of whether the audience of my comments consists of one or many students, I keep a copy of my responses with an assignment form. By doing so, I can save an enormous amount of time modifying and reusing my existing explanations or commentaries. The assignment form has been provided in the last section of this chapter.

Hutchinson (2007) uses a three-level marking system. At the first level, he looks at how well the student achieved and demonstrates a basic understanding of the activities involved in the assignment. For level two, Hutchinson analyzes the interaction that took place with the learning objectives and social environment. Level three consists of checking for a demonstrated coherent understanding that is supported with life experiences or examples. The assessment techniques at the end of this chapter provide both similar and different approaches to Hutchinson's three levels.

Deliver Feedback and Results to Students

Aside from letting students know that I am still present in the virtual environment, the main purpose I use feedback is to supply students with information that will guide the learning process by correcting misconceptions and moving students to the next level of learning. In a study performed by Lewis and Sewell (2007), students exhibited a desire for feedback and many would like to be provided with even more feedback than they actually get. For feedback to be effective, it needs to be timely, preferably immediate (Gaytan and McEwen 2007); it should consist of practical and productive information, with the instructor taking care not to be negative (Coats 2002); and it requires the use of consistent responses (James et al. 2002). Group feedback is helpful and efficient, but individual feedback that directly addresses a particular student's performance and learning on specific assignments or test questions is also required (James et al. 2002).

I have found the feedback practice to be a critical but very time-consuming portion of the assessment process. To address this issue, I tend to provide less feedback on items that demonstrate the level of learning stated in my objectives. My feedback to students in this category acknowledges that I reviewed their work and confirms that the students appear to be on track. Only a few words are necessary. For students who appear to be still struggling to meet my objectives, I take more time to supply a greater depth of feedback.

According to Gaytan and McEwen (2007), online assessments require an approach that is more systematic and continuous than traditional classroom assessments. While the demand for continuous assessment results in a high volume of assessment activity, not all products require even a confirmation each time they are reviewed, such as journals and learning logs. Carr (2002) recommends the development of a schedule to ensure that these products are used as part of the assessment process and not forgotten.

Assessment Techniques

The instructor's choice of assessment techniques will vary with the type of information or activity being assessed, as well as the purpose of the assessment. In this section, I have included several quick assessment techniques from Angelo and Cross (1993) that I revised for the online environment. For lengthier performance-based activities, I have provided an assessment instrument that contains established criteria to discover whether specific learning functions have occurred and the depth of learning that took place.

Quick Assessment

Prior Knowledge

When beginning a new unit, a starting point in the content must be decided. Rather than waste time teaching what has already been learned, I like to assess prior knowledge of the subject. As a result of the time saved, I can revise my goals to a higher level of understanding or move on to a new topic altogether. Prior knowledge can be assessed by the use of pretests (Price and Randall 2008). Grades, of course, are not assigned to pretest activities. Instead, I let students know the purpose of the pretest and that the results will be used to begin the course at an appropriate level. According to Angelo and Cross (1993), the pretest can take the form of open-ended questions, brief questionnaires, or quizzes with multiple-choice response options. I most frequently use two to five open-ended questions, depending upon the topic. Because it is a type of test, I direct my students in an online environment to place their responses in a private forum or dropbox. In my courses, I use the pretest method only in areas where I suspect a diverse knowledge base or to verify my expectations that the topic is commonly understood.

Minute Paper

To assess what was learned and/or what more the student would like to know, I adapted the minute paper technique listed by Angelo and Cross (1993). Depending upon what I am trying to assess, such as content in an online "lecture," instructional activity, or media used, I will often request feedback by asking "What was the most important thing that you learned from . . . ," with the blank filled in with the particular engagement. I sometimes ask a second question, "What questions do you still have?"

What's the Principle?

After the class has learned principles in a unit, I ask students to identify particular principles in scenarios I create or to use the principles to solve a problem. Responses are then placed in the dropbox labeled for this assessment.

Discussion Boards and Forums

Communication helps build a collaborative and cooperative environment, fostering student engagement and teamwork, and can be achieved by using distance learning tools such as discussion boards, also called forums, or chat rooms. This technology allows the instructor to conduct case studies, brainstorming, role-playing, critiques, and reaction or position papers (Hazari 2004).

I have never developed a course without the realization that there is much to teach and little time. When developing learning activities, I want to ensure that both the students and I will be able to manage the course demands. I recognize that for every assignment used, I must review all submissions, moderate to keep the focus on the main idea, and frequently provide feedback. For this reason, I proceed with caution.

To get the most benefit from forum discussion, I provide my students with the assignment criteria and also a model of the response expected. By doing so, I am paving the way for rich discussions that will meet the established goals, whether the purpose is to build a community, increase knowledge and understanding, or discover students' values and attitudes. In other words, the quality of the response, rather than the frequency, is what I assess.

In Table 10.1, I have provided a rubric for marking or scoring students' discussion contributions. This rubric is an abbreviated version of Hazari's (2004) hybrid approach that was devised by merging portions of several different methods. With the inclusion of a field for the learning objective, I can prevent vaguely written objectives and store related information in one location to ensure that I properly evaluate what I stated would be assessed. In order to verify the correlation between the learning objective and instructional activity, I added a field to identify and describe the coordinating assignment.

As a result of reducing the number of criteria listed in Hazari's rubric to only those I deemed the most important, I can perform the assessment quickly. I retained Hazari's rubric scale of 1.0 to 5.0 points, using increments of .5, but not all discussions or forums will be ranked 1.0 to 5.0. For example, one assignment I conduct is focused on building a community. I have the students post a response to the question, "If your house caught fire and you had time to save only one item, what item would you save

Table 10.1

Discussion Rubric

Learning objective	Assignment	
Scale	Criteria	Score
1.0–2.0 Participates	Responded by due date Opinion only Constructive comments Completeness	
3.0–4.0	Relevant responses Constructive feedback Examples	
5.0	Cited research or other sources and/or New perspectives and/or Strategic knowledge	

Source: Adapted from Hazari (2004, 351).

and why?" Then students are asked to consider another student's response and to decide whether, if they owned the same item, they would change their mind and save that item or keep with their original choice.

A different lens would be required for each discussion that coincides with the purpose or objectives of the assignment. In the previous example, I would set the value of the assignment in the 1.0 to 2.0 point range. I would not evaluate the correctness of the item chosen but instead focus on the completeness of the submission, checking if all parts of the question were addressed and reading the constructive comments in order to judge whether the assignment showed consideration or if the student appeared to have just gone through the motions.

Rubric Assignment Instrument

On the Internet, there are numerous free rubric generators or prefabricated rubrics. Unfortunately, I can quickly lose my focus when creating a rubric to assess the learning level of an objective unless I follow the framework provided by Anderson and Krathwohl's (2001) revision of Bloom's taxonomy of educational objectives. In Table 10.2, I altered Anderson and Krathwohl's revised taxonomy table by making it a form that could be used when assessing the learning of a performance-based activity requiring students to engage in more in-depth tasks or take more time to complete than other assignments. Once again, by incorporating a field for the learning objective, I can prevent vaguely written objectives and store related information in one location to ensure that I properly evaluate what I stated would be assessed. In order to verify the correlation between the learning objective and instructional activity, I added a field to identify and describe the coordinating assignment. The blank fields intersecting the knowledge dimension and cognitive process can be used in various ways. Marks or points can be added to indicate the highest level of knowledge demonstrated in the assignment. Another option would be to copy evidence directly from the student's product to the coordinating field, adding in the ability to quickly check for consistency or when scoring questions arise. The form fields could also be used to record standardized comments that could be modified and reused to individualize the feedback.

Key terminologies for knowledge dimensions to be used in conjunction with this form are (Armstrong 2009):

- Factual knowledge—knowledge of terminology, knowledge of specific details and elements
- Conceptual knowledge—knowledge of classifications and categories, knowledge of principles and generalizations, knowledge of theories, models, and structures
- Procedural knowledge—knowledge of subject-specific skills and algorithms, knowledge of subject-specific techniques and methods, knowledge of criteria for determining when to use appropriate procedures
- Metacognitive knowledge—strategic knowledge; knowledge about cognitive tasks, including appropriate contextual and conditional knowledge; self-knowledge

Words that provide an in-depth description for each of the six cognitive processes were supplied by Anderson and Krathwohl (2001) to guide the assessment process. An abbreviated version of the action list is:

1. Remember—recall, list, define
2. Understand—explain, demonstrate, summarize
3. Apply—discuss, model
4. Analyze—classify, categorize, compare
5. Evaluate—speculate, judge, interpret, dispute
6. Create—design, generate, reconstruct

Table 10.2

Revised Taxonomy Form

Learning objective	Instructional activity name and description Student/Group					
	Cognitive process					
Knowledge dimension	Remember	Understand	Apply	Analyze	Evaluate	Create
Factual:						
Conceptual:						
Procedural						
Metacognitive						

Source: Adapted from Anderson and Krathwohl (2001).

Conclusion

For both students and faculty, learning is the expected outcome of any course. It should remain foremost in the instructor's consideration as courses are developed and as they proceed. From start to finish, the assessment process can be a large and time-consuming task, requiring a systematic plan, but the payoffs are even greater.

Whether in a traditional or virtual classroom environment, assessing learning is a requirement for effective teaching and learning. If the end result desired is to revise instructional methods in order to improve learning, then the formative method of assessment must be used on a continual basis. Regardless of the assessment technique used, a valid assessment occurs when a correlation exists between the criteria used to evaluate learning and the established course objectives. Armed with the assessment information and examples provided in this chapter, an educator should now be ready to go forth and assess.

References

Anderson, Lorin W., and David R. Krathwohl, eds. 2001. *A Taxonomy for Learning, Teaching, and Assessing: A Revision of Bloom's Taxonomy of Educational Objectives.* New York: Longman.

Angelo, Thomas A., and K. Patricia Cross. 1993. *Classroom Assessment Techniques: A Handbook for College Teachers.* 2nd ed. San Francisco: Jossey-Bass.

Armstrong, Patricia. 2009. "Bloom's Taxonomy." Center for Teaching, Vanderbilt University. www.vanderbilt.edu/cft/resources/teaching_resources/theory/blooms.htm#2001.

Asselin, M. 2003. "Assessment Issues and Recommendations." *Teacher Librarian* 30, no. 5: 52.

Bloom, Benjamin S. and David R. Krathwohl, eds. 1956. *Taxonomy of Educational Objectives: The Classification of Educational Goals, by a Committee of College and University Examiners. Handbook 1: Cognitive Domain.* New York: Longmans, Green.

Carr, Sonya C. 2002. "Assessing Learning Processes: Useful Information for Teachers and Students." *Intervention in School and Clinic* 37, no. 3: 156–162.

Christopher, Mary M., Julie A. Thomas, and Mary K. Tallent-Runnels. 2004. "Raising the Bar: Encouraging High Level Thinking in Online Discussion Forums." *Roeper Review* 26, no. 3: 166–171.

Coats, Maggie 2002. "Enhancing Student Learning Through the Assessment of Outcomes: Developing and Demonstrating Essay Writing Skills." Paper presented at the Association for the Study of Evaluation in Education in South Africa (ASEESA) Conference, Johannesburg, South Africa, July. www.open.ac.uk/cobe/docs/publications/ASEESA2002.pdf.

Colburn, Alan 2009. "The Prepared Practitioner." *Science Teacher* 76, no. 2: 10–11.

Fairfield-Sonn, James W., Bharat Kolluri, Annette Rogers, and Rao Singamsetti. 2009. "Enhancing an Undergraduate Business Statistics Course: Linking Teaching and Learning with Assessment Issues." *American Journal of Business Education* 2, no. 7: 101–112.

Fink, L. Dee. 2003. *Creating Significant Learning Experiences: An Integrated Approach to Designing College Courses.* San Francisco: Jossey-Bass.

Gaytan, Jorge, and Beryl C. McEwen. 2007. "Effective Online Instructional and Assessment Strategies." *American Journal of Distance Education* 21, no. 3: 117–132.

Gerretson, Helen, and Emily Golson. 2005. "Synopsis of the Use of Course-Embedded Assessment in a Medium Sized Public University's General Education Program." *Journal of General Education* 54, no. 2: 139–149.

Hazari, Sunil 2004. "Strategy for Assessment of Online Course Discussions." *Journal of Information Systems Education* 15, no. 4: 349–355.

Hutchinson, Damien. 2007. "Teaching Practices for Effective Cooperative Learning in an Online Learning Environment (OLE)." *Journal of Information Systems Education* 18, no. 3: 357–367.

Illinois Online Network. 2010. "Instructional Strategies for Online Courses." University of Illinois. www.ion.uillinois.edu/resources/tutorials/pedagogy/instructionalstrategies.asp.

James, Richard, Craig McInnis, Marcia Devlin, and AUTC. 2002. *Assessing Learning in Australian Universities.* Canberra: Australian Universities Teaching Committee. www.cshe.unimelb.edu.au/assessinglearning/docs/AssessingLearning.pdf.

Lei, Simon A. 2008. "Assessment Techniques of Instructors in Two Community Colleges in a State-Wide System." *Education* 128, no. 3: 392–411.

Lewis, David J.A., and Robert D.E. Sewell. 2007. "Providing Formative Feedback from a Summative Computer-Aided Assessment." *American Journal of Pharmaceutical Education* 71, no. 2: 33. www.ncbi.nlm.nih.gov/pmc/articles/PMC1858616.

Liang, Xin, and Kim Creasy. 2004. "Classroom Assessment in Web-Based Instructional Environment: Instructors' Experience." *Practical Assessment, Research and Evaluation* 9, no. 7. http://pareonline.net/getvn.asp?v=9&n=7.

Magnussen, Lois. 2008. "Applying the Principles of Significant Learning in the E-Learning Environment." *Journal of Nursing Education* 47, no. 2: 82–85.

Marriott, Pru. 2009. "Students' Evaluation of the Use of Online Summative Assessment in an Undergraduate Financial Accounting Module." *British Journal of Educational Technology* 40, no. 2: 237–254.

Palmer, Stuart, Dale Holt, and Sharyn Bray. 2008. "Does the Discussion Help? The Impact of a Formally Assessed Online Discussion on Final Student Results." *British Journal of Educational Technology* 39, no. 5: 847–858.

Price, Barbara A., and Cindy H. Randall. 2008. "Assessing Learning Outcomes in Quantitative Courses: Using Embedded Questions for Direct Assessment." *Journal of Education for Business* 83, no. 5: 288–294.

Quality Assurance Agency (QAA). 2006. *Section 6: Assessment of Students.* www.qaa.ac.uk/academicinfrastructure/codeOfPractice/default.asp.

Rogers, Gloria. 2006. "Assessment 101: Direct and Indirect Assessments: What Are They Good For?" *ABET Community Matters* 3–4 (August). www.abet.org/Linked Documents-UPDATE/Newsletters/06-08-CM.pdf.

Wells, Jason. 2006. "Markers Assistant: A Software Solution for the Management of the Assessment Process." *International Journal on Elearning* 5, no. 3: 439–458.

$$\boxed{11}$$

Creating an Environment of
Faculty Involvement

Steven J. Hoffman

It seems clear to anybody who is paying attention that teaching online has both promise and peril. Even a quick look at the numerous studies conducted on online education reveals that faculty involvement with online teaching contains risk. Faculty members risk losing engagement and interaction with students in the online environment, spending a lot of time that is unrecognized and unrewarded, and experiencing massive levels of technologically induced frustration. But these same studies also highlight much potential reward: faculty members involved in online education report high degrees of satisfaction in the prospect of reaching students who might not otherwise be able to take a class, engaging and interacting with students in new and exciting ways as they pursue their own learning, and being on the cutting edge of developing new pedagogies for teaching and learning in the twenty-first century.[1]

Despite the perils and prospects for individual faculty members, however, one thing seems abundantly clear: higher education is increasingly moving in the direction of providing more and more online courses. According to the Sloan Consortium's reports on online education in the United States, the percentage of schools' chief academic officers identifying online education as "critical to the long-term strategy of their school" increased steadily from 48.8 percent in 2002 to 59.1 percent in 2006, where it seems to have reached a plateau, varying less than 1 percent between 2005 and 2009 (Allen and Seaman 2007, 16; 2010, 10). The 2009 report noted that student enrollment in at least one online course increased from 1.6 million in fall 2002 to 4.6 million in fall 2008. This rate of increase represents a compound annual growth rate of 19 percent at a time when the entire student body experienced a growth rate of only

1.5 percent. According to the Sloan survey, in fall 2008 "students taking at least one online course now represent more than 25 percent of total enrollments in higher education" (Allen and Seaman 2010, 5). Clearly, online education is a growing part of the higher education landscape. The only question that remains is who is going to develop and teach all these courses?

Despite roughly similar rates of current participation in online teaching, if tenured and tenure-track faculty members do not wish to be displaced by adjunct and non-tenure-track faculty, they will have to continue to increase their involvement. A 2005 Sloan Consortium report suggested that "there [was] a slightly greater use of core faculty for teaching online than for face-to-face" courses; however, this trend looks like it is beginning to change. According to Sloan, in 2005 "sixty-five percent of higher education institutions report[ed] that they [were] using primarily core faculty to teach their online courses compared to 62 percent that report[ed] they [were] using primarily core faculty to teach their face-to-face courses." The evidence suggested that "except for the largest schools (15000+ enrollment), all sized schools report[ed] an equal or greater rate of online courses being taught primarily by core faculty compared to their face-to-face courses" (Allen and Seaman 2005, overview). A 2009 survey, however, reveals that "part-time faculty are more likely to engage in online learning than their full-time counterparts, with 32.4 percent of part-time faculty currently teaching online compared to 22.2 percent of full-timers." Looking at the rates of participation for faculty who have ever taught online, however, the difference is much smaller, with 39.7 percent for part-timers compared to 33.6 percent for full-time faculty. This suggests that although "all types of faculty teach online in roughly similar proportions . . . part-time and non-tenure track [faculty] do so with greater frequency" (Seaman 2009, 15).

Motivating Faculty to Teach Online

So what are the elements needed in order to promote an environment of faculty involvement in creating effective online courses? What do faculty members need to have in place in order to maximize the likelihood of success? Faculty participation in online education appears to be steadily rising. A 2003 report suggested "between two and twelve percent of faculty [were] already engaged in some form of teaching via technology beyond the campus proper" (Daba 2003). In 2009, a Sloan

Foundation survey found that "over one-third (34.4 percent) of faculty have taught online" and that "nearly one-quarter of all faculty responding (23.6 percent) were teaching at least one online course at the time of the survey" (Seaman 2009, 5). In terms of the Rogers model for adoption and diffusion of innovation, the growth of online teaching has spread beyond the innovators and early adopters to include part of the early majority (Rogers 2003).[2] The question for most institutions is how to continue increasing that spread.

It helps to understand why faculty members choose to teach online. Typically rewards for developing online courses can generally be classified as either intrinsic or extrinsic, ranging from such things as self-satisfaction and flexibility to external recognition, additional payments, and release time. As important as these factors are in motivating faculty members to venture online, however, addressing the disincentives that may keep faculty members from doing so is also necessary. These disincentives range from the increased time for preparation to a lack of recognition for their work. In the final analysis, however, studies show that faculty members are, not surprisingly, motivated to teach online for the same reasons they are motivated to teach face-to-face classes (Bruner 2007; Parker 2003; Schifter 2004).

So how do schools translate this understanding into institutional practice that will enable them to involve more faculty members in teaching online successfully? First and foremost, what is needed is significant, concrete support at the university level. The most tangible support comes in the form of training. Studies have shown that effective online courses require much more than faculty members simply placing their face-to-face class notes on the web. Creating effective learning opportunities for students online involves learning about both technological and pedagogical techniques that differ from the techniques faculty members might use in a face-to-face classroom (Kim and Bonk 2006; Sixl-Daniell, Williams, and Wong 2006; Yang and Cornelious 2005).

Training

To help faculty make the transition between face-to-face and online teaching, Southeast Missouri State University (Southeast), like many institutions, offers a series of technology workshops on topics ranging from website development and using PowerPoint to producing streaming audio and video lectures. Since 1997, Southeast's Center for Scholarship in Teaching and

Learning (CSTL), the faculty development office on campus, has offered over 554 workshops attended by over 7,033 faculty members. Of course, that figure represents some faculty attending more than one workshop. In fact, the record for attendance by a single faculty member is 148 workshops by a faculty member in the College of Business. Nonetheless, the overall reach of the workshops has been enormous. The unduplicated head count for all technology workshops since 1997 is 899, which, out of a faculty of approximately 400, suggests a pretty good representation (Phillips 2010).

It is important to note that this commitment does not come cheap. The CSTL's budget for workshops alone is about $70,000 annually, which covers the cost of food, facilitator stipends, materials (software, books, etc.), and the student workers who support the faculty (Starrett 2010). But for faculty members, having this training available is an essential prerequisite for making the leap into teaching online. One study reported that "four out of the five obstacles" listed by faculty as impediments to teaching online suggest "that faculty tend to see distance education as a *time demanding activity that requires new skill development*" (Seaman 2009, 33–35; Rockwell et al. 1999). Workshop training is vital to addressing this concern.

But technical training is only part of the equation. Unless faculty members are supported in their efforts to learn and employ new pedagogical techniques in their online classrooms, their courses will be mediocre at best. As numerous studies have shown, faculty need to understand that teaching online is different from teaching face-to-face. To help faculty members understand this, all new online faculty should be exposed to what it feels like to learn online. At Southeast, new online faculty are required to complete a two-week online workshop titled Teaching in the Online Environment. Since 2001, the workshop has been offered once or twice a year and 234 faculty members have taken it so far (Phillips 2010). The workshop addresses many of the differences between teaching online and face-to-face. More important, however, it provides faculty members with their own experience of taking an online course. Online faculty get a heavy dose of being a student: waiting to hear from the professors about their grades, wondering if the teacher is listening when they post, trying to navigate the site to find the next assignment, scrolling through pages that are too long. The workshop facilitators intentionally leave "mistakes" in the class so that the soon-to-be-online instructors get to feel what students feel when, for example, scheduled quizzes are not available by the due date. Ultimately the workshop is designed to model effective techniques for teaching online, expose instructors to potential problems their students might experience, and provide instructors with a learning community of fellow online professors with whom to share ideas and techniques. There is nothing like trying to learn online to give instructors a better sense of what they need to do to be able to teach online effectively (Sixl-Daniell, Williams, and Wong 2006).

Incentives

Of course, we all know that giving faculty the right tools to teach effectively online is only part of the answer to getting them involved in developing online courses. Faculty members also need incentive. Some will develop online courses just because teaching online is a new, exciting challenge, but in order to get faculty truly involved, institutions need to provide incentives. Incentives can come in a variety of forms, and although studies show cash is not necessarily the most effective reward, it does work, alas, they say, given in small amounts for a limited time and a specific objective. In essence, cash is a "good enough" "short term" motivator (Deci, Koestner, and Ryan 2001; Tobias 2004).

Ultimately, for most faculty members, deciding to teach online comes down to a question of either time or money. Several studies of faculty motivation suggest that institutions should consider adjusting the workload of online course developers because of the perception that developing and teaching an online course takes more time than developing and teaching a face-to-face class, thus increasing faculty resistance to getting involved. One study showed "that institutions that do offer course reductions for such faculty members are successful in motivating them" to develop online courses. Yet, as Giannoni and Tesone found, "other research results uncovered from an NEA study showed that eighty-four percent of instructors do not receive this incentive" (Giannoni and Tesone 2003; see also Bower 2001; Schifter 2000).

Of course, as we all know, what instructors really desire is some kind of recognition for their effort. Although cash may not be the best overall incentive, it is by far easier for institutions to give than other, more meaningful rewards (Chizmar and Williams 2001). To this end, at Southeast, a faculty member receives $1,500 to develop a course to be delivered online. Between 1999 and 2004, more than $180,000 was distributed to about 100 faculty members to develop approximately 125 courses, an investment that rose to over $253,000 in development costs alone by 2010 (Grebing 2010).

Another incentive available to faculty at Southeast, and very attractive to some, is a virtual promise of summer teaching. After all, who can argue with teaching a course from the beach! Studies show that "the concept of faculty flexibility is a particularly significant factor in motivating professors to teach via distance media, particularly with asynchronous forms," or, in other words, online (Clay 1999). Although I have been clearly instructed by the dean who oversees Southeast Online, our online division at the university, that there is no "promise" of summer teaching, it seems clear that being able to teach an online course or two makes it much more likely that a faculty member will have the chance to teach during the summer. Part of the summer budget is devoted to summer salaries for online courses, approximately \$173,350 in the summer of 2009. Faculty are limited to teaching two courses, whether face-to-face, online, or both. In the department of history, we have a small budget for face-to-face classes, and rotating through the list of faculty results in the opportunity for each instructor to teach a summer class every three years or so. However, if instructors can offer an online class, chances are they can offer it every summer. We have had four faculty members who have been able to teach in the summer without regard to where they are on the summer rotation list because the online budget is separate from the face-to-face budget, at least for the time being. There is, of course, some idle speculation that the university is moving toward offering only online courses during the summer, but we are probably a few years away from that. In summer 2009 we had 142 courses delivered online, representing 20.43 percent of the total for-credit courses offered. These courses, however, represented almost 42.12 percent of the number of credit hours generated, making them financially attractive to university administrators and students alike (Grebing 2010). It is hard to know whether those hours are those borrowed or stolen from the regular semester or whether they are hours we simply would not have had without the online courses. Probably they are both, although the dean overseeing the delivery of online courses indicates that we have some evidence that they lean to the latter. Regardless, for our faculty, the chance to earn extra money in the summer has become one of the incentives we currently offer to develop and deliver their courses online.

Technology Support for Faculty

In addition to providing training and incentives, it is important that the institution provide ongoing technology support for faculty teaching online. Even faculty who are innovators will run into problems and questions and they will need access to high-quality technology support if the institution is to sustain a high-quality online program. To move beyond the innovators (2.5 percent) and early adopters (13.5 percent) to reach the early majority (34 percent), let alone the late majority (34 percent) and the laggards (16 percent), requires a substantial commitment to ongoing technical support for faculty members who take the leap. In essence, if the early adopters are successful and cared for, they will be the recruiters of the early majority. Overcoming what some studies have identified as "technological anxiety" over teaching in the online environment is key to overall success (Giannoni and Tesone 2003; Rogers 2003).

At Southeast, the CSTL has a solid reputation as a faculty-friendly, very helpful office that does much to reduce technological anxiety on the part of the teaching faculty. It has staff on call to answer questions and do design work for both online and blended courses using technology in the face-to-face classroom. The CSTL currently has one three-quarter-time director, one half-time assistant director/faculty associate, one full-time web manager, one half-time web manager, three full-time technology support staff, one full-time instructional designer, two graduate assistants who work twenty hours a week, six student technology consultants averaging ten to fifteen hours a week each, and one half-time administrative assistant with five student support staff members at ten to fifteen hours a week each. The CSTL is separate from the office for Southeast Online, which has its own director and student support staff (Starrett 2010). What this means for faculty is that help is just a phone call or an email away. Most faculty members have been hired for their expertise in some content area; few have expertise in education and even fewer in technology. By holding their hands and assisting them in the design and delivery of their courses, the CSTL staff is able to help instructors transition effectively into the online environment. Having strong technology support for faculty eliminates a potential barrier to faculty involvement in developing and teaching online courses (Rockwell et al. 1999).

Another, less important but not insignificant factor supporting the development and teaching of online courses at Southeast is the fact that CSTL staff members are also available to do some of the menial labor of moving materials online, from scanning images and text to creating streaming files. By taking over this drudgery, CSTL staffers allow the faculty members to focus on the pedagogical issues involved in creating an effective online experience for their students. Back in the early days, the CSTL supplied funding for a graduate student to scan all my architecture slides for use in an online architectural history class. More recently, when the textbooks did not reach our students in Iraq by the time the class started, CSTL staff scanned each chapter as a PDF file so the students could keep up with their work. Although most faculty members would be capable of accomplishing these tasks themselves, the job is much easier—and the online teaching experience more positive—when they do not have to do so. In addition, since one of the faculty concerns about venturing online is the expenditure of too much time, anything the institution can do to alleviate this burden will help eliminate one of the barriers to increased faculty involvement in teaching online.

A last area of technology support for faculty involves the course management system. At Southeast, we use a system developed in-house called the Online Instructor Suite (OIS). Although there is much debate about the wisdom of maintaining an in-house system versus purchasing one of the major vendors' products, from a faculty perspective the OIS has its positive attributes. Although Blackboard and WebCt have their supporters and although maintaining a system in-house is not without risk, being able to request changes to the software to accommodate professors' needs is a plus that is not available from commercial vendors, at least not with the kind of rapid response we get from the CSTL staff. Regardless of the course management system used, however, the bottom line is that faculty members teaching online need to be able to contact someone to resolve problems with a reasonable expectation of a prompt, courteous, and competent response.

Technology Support for Students

In addition to technical support for faculty, the institution needs to have a robust system in place to provide technical support for students; otherwise, instructors will be spending all their time answering questions about how to get the technology to work and not have any time to answer questions or provide feedback to students on the actual course content. The hours spent troubleshooting why a streaming file plays fine on the instructor's computer, but will not load on a student's are hours that would have been better spent providing feedback to student posts in the discussion forum. Regardless of the system in place to deal with students' technology problems, faculty members will often be called on as first responders to put out the fires of technology-induced disasters.

It is helpful to be able to refer most of those questions to a competent technical support staff and then simply monitor the situation to ensure that the students' problems are resolved. Although there is a help page on the Southeast Online website in the form of FAQ pages (http://online.semo. edu/content/FAQ.asp) to help students solve common problems, it seems pretty obvious, based on some of the questions students pose, that students do not always avail themselves of these. The instructional technology (IT) desk can do simple online course troubleshooting as well. With a common portal as the entry point into online courses, password, access, and connectivity problems for the most part can go through the campus IT desk rather than through a special online course support office. But having support staff who, at least theoretically, have a greater appreciation for the teaching focus of the technology is critical to a successful online teaching experience, an appreciation normally not available from the typical college IT help desk. In most cases, the instructor ends up providing a portion of the technology support students need.

Copyright Issues: Who Owns an Online Course?

One of the last university-level issues that needs to be addressed revolves around the question of copyright: who owns the online course, the faculty member or the institution? Although faculty members may not be accustomed to thinking of their work in these terms, publishing a course on the university server requires a clear understanding of the implications for all involved. Faculty members should ask if the university has a written policy about this issue or if there is just a general understanding. Lack of clarity about copyright issues has been identified as a possible barrier to getting faculty involved in developing online courses, and it may be an issue that an institution should resolve before its instructors go online (Bruner 2007; Giannoni and Tesone 2003; McCarthy 2009, 36; Starrett 2004).

At Southeast, established policy suggests that the faculty member owns any course materials created or developed, unless a specific contract was signed giving dual ownership to the university. The issue of course ownership first arose when Southeast began offering stipends to develop online courses, leading some faculty members to believe that it would change the course into a "work for hire" that would then belong to the university, lock, stock, and syllabus. So far, however, such has not been the case. We still defer to the faculty handbook, which, in the absence of a specific contract specifying otherwise, gives outright ownership of online course content solely to the developer—that is, the faculty member. The university owns the course management system and any course graphics it creates as well as the actual course syllabus, including its content. But the syllabus for the course, which tends to be a generic outline indicating the content that is to be covered, is not the same as an individual faculty member's syllabus for the class covering that material in any given semester. In other words, the university owns the course American History II, which covers the period from 1877 to the present, but the faculty member owns the particular syllabus and class materials developed to teach it. The stipends currently being offered by the university do not make the development of an online course a work for hire unless expressly stated in the contract. In a few cases, dual ownership has been agreed to and is specified in the contract—the faculty member owns the content, and so does the university—and the stipend for those courses is the same. The standard default contract, however, does not contain this clause, so faculty members still own their courses outright. This practice is, apparently, in the minority by a good margin nationally. The vast majority of online courses operate under dual ownership, although some are owned outright by the institution (McCarthy 2009, 36–37; Twigg 2000). Southeast recently developed a new online teaching contract that confirms faculty ownership of all online course materials produced, while at the same time allowing the university to teach the course for a maximum of two semesters in the event that the faculty member is no longer able to teach it for whatever reason (http://online. semo.edu/content/OnlineClassOwnershipProcedure.pdf). This protects the ability of the university to offer courses listed in the schedule and that students might need, while at the same time ensuring that the university will not continue to offer a faculty member's class in perpetuity without the owner's permission.

Departmental Support

Although university-level support is critical to successfully engaging faculty members in developing online classes, generally speaking our work lives are organized not by universities, but by departments within the university. It is important that there be at least some support at the department level, because regardless of the degree of university support that exists, significant opposition at the department level can be fatal to a faculty member's career.

Teaching Load Considerations

One of the first areas in which the department has to support the online professor has to do with teaching load. If a professor is expected or encouraged to offer an online course during the regular semester, the department will have to work out whether it will be offered as an overload or as part of the faculty member's regular load. This is not as innocuous an issue as it might first appear. Some jealous, but technologically inept colleagues (we all probably know one, if not in our department, then somewhere down the hall) will whine about their not getting the chance for the additional money that comes with a teaching overload. Or, if the online course is taught in-load, other faculty members will assume the online course is just a gimmick to get out of the classroom and to spend more time at home. Until an instructor has developed and taught a quality online class, it can be difficult to truly understand the time commitment it takes. Sloan's 2009 faculty survey indicated "64 percent of faculty surveyed believe[d] that online learning takes more effort to teach; and almost 85 percent believe it takes more effort to develop online courses" (McCarthy 2009). Given this widespread perception about the required time commitment, it is important that the department chair recognizes and supports the online contribution to the department's overall teaching mission in order to prevent misunderstandings. Although this issue has not yet come up in our department, one faculty member who decided to have his class discussions for his face-to-face class take place in the online environment every other week endured widespread criticism for scamming the department and just using the technology as an excuse to get out of his fair share of the teaching. That faculty member has since moved on to another university.

Student Credit Hour Production

Another issue at the department level revolves around student credit hour production. At Southeast, departments are encouraged to cap their online courses at a maximum of twenty-five students. This is in keeping with national norms. Nationally, the average course cap is slightly higher, at thirty for undergraduate courses and twenty-eight for graduate courses. Although one study found the range to vary between 10 and 150 students, the cap with the most frequency (the mode) was 25 (Vilic 2004). At Southeast, similar face-to-face courses are capped at thirty-five.

There is enormous pressure on department chairs to maximize student hour production, sometimes leading to raising the number of students in a given class. Unless departments strive to keep the number of students in online classes low, however, they risk both the quality of the course offering and the incentive to the faculty member to teach it. It might be a small reward for teaching online, but grading ten fewer finals is at least something.

Promotion, Tenure, and Merit

Perhaps the most important consideration at the department level relates to promotion, tenure, and merit. Although faculty members certainly need university-level support in the promotion, tenure and merit process as well, how the department views the investment of time in online endeavors is critically important. If the university says that online classes are the way of the future, but the department as a whole rejects that notion as just further proof of the decline in standards of teaching by the rest of the college, a faculty member should be very careful. According to a recent study of chief academic officers, they believe that only about one-third of their faculty "accept the value and legitimacy of online education" (Allen and Seaman 2010, 3, 12–13).

This represents a huge potential problem. The university can provide a certain level of support, but whatever individual faculty members do will be interpreted by department promotion committees. At Southeast we have worked hard to create a climate in the university that would support faculty members' involvement with activities associated with teaching with technology. In 1999, an action team commissioned by the vice provost created a document to aid campus promotion and tenure committees in evaluating fairly faculty activities involving teaching and technology, and in 2004 the university officially adopted a campus definition of the teacher-scholar model acknowledging a wide variety of pursuits as scholarly acts, including presentations and articles on teaching, technology, and the disciplines (www.semo.edu/facultysenate/correspondence/index_16439.htm). Some of these university policies have been incorporated in departmental guidelines for promotion, tenure and merit, including new guidelines adopted by the history department. Those guidelines, in fact, have a category specifically identified for "articles and chapters resulting from scholarship consistent with the teacher-scholar model embraced by the university, including articles on teaching, service, outreach and/or historic preservation/public history." When these guidelines were passed, over much opposition, it seemed to be a good thing. For faculty members climbing the ladder of tenure, promotion, and merit, it is vitally important to know whether the department will view their expenditure of time to develop online courses as a good thing or a bad thing. Thanks to the new guidelines, converting the investment of time using technology in teaching into scholarship is recognized as in keeping with the university's model of the teacher-scholar. Many academics pay lip service to the notion of the teacher-scholar, but do not have any clear idea of what it really means. That is one of the reasons I was pleased with both the university's and department's adoption of a specific definition that would reward as scholarship activities related to "teaching, technology and the disciplines."

Although having clear guidelines is essential, having clear guidelines and having them fairly implemented are two entirely different things. Given that only one-third of faculty members nationally "accept the value and legitimacy of online education," an anti-technology backlash may develop in some departments (Allen and Seaman 2010, 3). In my own case, my departmental promotion committee noted that "some members of the committee expressed concern that the considerable emphasis he places on electronic technology as a tool for teaching and learning may interfere with communication of the subject matter of a course" (personal communication). Although after only a year's delay this opposition was successfully overcome, the department as a whole remains lukewarm in its support for faculty being involved in technology and teaching.

We all know, of course, that each faculty member's record of service needs to be evaluated on its own terms and that circumstances vary from institution to institution. However, it also seems clear that if we are going to move beyond the innovators and early adopters and attract the early majority—which we will need to do if we are going to sustain faculty involvement in the creation of future web courses—we must address this all-important issue (Bolger and Sprow 2002; Easley, Hoffman, and Rhodes 2005; Howard 2006; Seaman 2009, 33; Starrett 2004; Young 2002).

Conclusion

Why do people do what they do? Why do faculty members develop and teach online courses, and how do we get more of them to do so? The evidence suggests we need to provide the kinds of support described in this chapter so we can ensure that faculty members who do venture online are successful, and then we need to recognize and reward them when they are. In time, the rest will follow.

Notes

1. For a beginning sample of the literature, see McCarthy (2009); Jaschik (2009); Bruner (2007); Schifter (2004); Parker (2003); Starrett (2004); and Easley, Hoffman, and Rhodes (2005).

2. In his groundbreaking work on the adoption of innovation, first published in 1962, Rogers theorizes that innovations spread through society in a predictable pattern based upon the standard bell curve and that people can be categorized into the following groups: innovators (2.5 percent), early adopters (13.5 percent), early majority (34 percent), late majority (34 percent), and laggards (16 percent).

References

Allen, I. Elaine, and Jeff Seaman. 2005. *Growing by Degrees: Online Education in the United States, 2005*. Sloan Consortium. November. www.sloan-c.org/publications/survey/growing_by_degrees_2005.

———. 2007. *Online Nation: Five Years of Growth in Online Learning*. Sloan Consortium. October. www.sloan-c.org/publications/survey/online_nation.

———. 2010. *Learning on Demand: Online Education in the United States, 2009*. Sloan Consortium. January. www.sloan-c.org/publications/survey/learning_on_demand_sr2010.

Bolger, Dorita F., and Richard L. Sprow. 2002. "Technology-Based Projects in Performance and/or Promotion and Tenure Decisions in Liberal Arts Colleges." Paper presented at EDUCAUSE Conference, Teaching, Technology, and Tenure: How Are They Valued? Atlanta, GA, October. http://net.educause.edu/ir/library/pdf/EDU0221a.pdf.

Bower, Beverley L. 2001. "Distance Education: Facing the Faculty Challenge." *Online Journal of Distance Learning Administration* 4, no. 2. www.westga.edu/~distance/ojdla/summer42/bower42.html.

Bruner, John. 2007. "Factors Motivating and Inhibiting Faculty in Offering Their Courses via Distance Education." *Online Journal of Distance Learning Administration* 10, no. 2. www.westga.edu/~distance/ojdla/summer102/bruner102.htm.

Chizmar, John F., and David B. Williams. 2001. "What Do Faculty Want?" *EDUCAUSE Quarterly* 1. www.educause.edu/ir/library/pdf/eqm0112.pdf.

Clay, Melanie. 1999. "Development of Training and Support Programs for Distance Education Instructors." *Online Journal of Distance Learning Administration* 2, no. 3. www.westga.edu/~distance/clay23.html.

Daba, Farhad. 2003. "The Future of Distance Education: Research, Conceptual Development and Practice." Paper presented at the 19th Annual Conference on Distance Teaching and Learning, July. Madison, WI www.uwex.edu/disted/conference/Resource_library/proceedings/03_29.pdf.

Deci, Edward L., Richard Koestner, and Richard M. Ryan. 2001. "Extrinsic

Rewards and Intrinsic Motivation in Education: Reconsidered Once Again." *Review of Educational Research* 71, no 1: 1–27. www.psych.rochester.edu/SDT/documents/2001_DeciKoestnerRyan.pdf.

Easley, Larry, Steven Hoffman, and Joel Rhodes. 2005. "Warning! Technology Can Be Dangerous to Your Health: A Case Study from the Trenches." *Journal of the Association for History and Computing* 8, no. 1. http://mcel.pacificu.edu/jahc/2005/issue1/articles/easley.php.

Giannoni, Dawn, and Dana V. Tesone. 2003. "What Academic Administrators Should Know to Attract Senior Level Faculty Members to Online Learning Environments." *Online Journal of Distance Learning Administration* 7, no. 1. www.westga.edu/~distance/ojdla/spring61/giannoni61.htm.

Grebing, Robin. 2010. Director, Southeast Online Programs, email to author, March 5.

Howard, Jennifer. 2006. "The Talk of the MLA: Technology, Teaching, and Politics." *Chronicle of Higher Education*, January 13.

Jaschik, Scott. 2009. "The Evidence on Online Education." *Inside Higher Ed*, June 29. www.insidehighered.com/layout/set/print/news/2009/06/29/online.

Kim, Kyong-Jee, and Curtis J. Bonk. 2006. "The Future of Online Teaching and Learning in Higher Education: The Survey Says . . ." *EDUCAUSE Quarterly* 4: 22–30.

McCarthy, Sally A. 2009. *Online Learning as a Strategic Asset*, vol. 1: *A Resource for Campus Leaders*. Association of Public and Land-Grant Universities. August. www.sloanconsortium.org/sites/default/files/APLU_online_strategic_asset_vol1-1_1.pdf.

Parker, Angie. 2003. "Motivation and Incentives for Distance Faculty." *Online Journal of Distance Learning Administration* 6, no. 3. www.westga.edu/~distance/ojdla/fall63/parker63.htm.

Phillips, Sondra. 2010. Center for Scholarship in Teaching and Learning, Southeast Missouri State University, email message to author, February 16.

Rockwell, S. Kay, Jolene Schauer, Susan M. Fritz, and David B. Marx. 1999. "Incentives and Obstacles Influencing Higher Education Faculty and Administrators to Teach Via Distance." *Online Journal of Distance Learning Administration* 2, no. 3. www.westga.edu/~distance/rockwell24.html.

Rogers, Everett M. 2003. *Diffusion of Innovations*. 5th ed. New York: Free Press.

Schifter, Catherine C. 2000. "Faculty Participation in Asynchronous Learning Networks: A Case Study of Motivating and Inhibiting Factors." *Journal of Asynchronous Learning Networks* 4, no 1. www.westga.edu/~distance/ojdla/spring121/maguire121.html.

———. 2004. "Compensation Models in Distance Education: National Survey Questionnaire Revisited." *Online Journal of Distance Learning Administration* 7, no. 1. www.westga.edu/~distance/ojdla/spring71/schifter71.html.

Seaman, Jeff. 2009. *Online Learning as a Strategic Asset*, vol. 2: *The Paradox of Faculty Voices: Views and Experiences with Online Learning*. Association of Public and Land-Grant Universities. August. www.sloanconsortium.org/sites/default/files/APLU_online_strategic_asset_vol2-1.pdf.

Sixl-Daniell, Karin, Jeremy B. Williams, and Amy Wong. 2006. "A Quality Assurance Framework for Recruiting, Training (and Retaining) Virtual Adjunct Faculty." *Online Journal of Distance Learning Administration* 9, no. 9. www.westga.edu/~distance/ojdla/spring91/daniell91.htm.

Starrett, David. 2004. "Faculty & Technology: Rewarding TET." *Campus Technology*, October 1. http://campustechnology.com/articles/2004/09/faculty-technology-rewarding-tet.aspx.

———. 2010. Director, Center for Scholarship in Teaching and Learning, Southeast Missouri State University, email message to author, February 15.

Tobias, Suzanne Perez. 2004. "Cash Rewards." *Arizona Republic*, October 13. www.azcentral.com/families/articles/1013fam_cashrewards.html.

Twigg, Carol A. 2000. *Who Owns Online Courses and Course Materials? Intellectual Property Policies for a New Learning Environment*. Pew Learning and Technology Program. www.thencat.org/Monographs/Whoowns.html.

Vilic, Boris. 2004. "Online Course Caps: A Survey." *Syllabus* (July/August). http://campustechnology.com/articles/2004/06/online-course-caps-a-survey.aspx?sc_lang=en.

Yang, Yi, and Linda F. Cornelious. 2005. "Preparing Instructors for Quality Online Instruction." *Online Journal of Distance Learning Administration* 7, no. 1. www.westga.edu/~distance/ojdla/spring81/yang81.htm.

Young, Jeffrey R. 2002. "Ever So Slowly, Colleges Start to Count Work with Technology in Tenure Decisions." *Chronicle of Higher Education*, February 22.

If the Future Is Now, What Is Next?

Five Trends Affecting the Future of Online Education

David J. Staley

Online education is not a passing fad, at least for now. The Sloan Consortium's 2009 survey *Learning on Demand*, and indeed the other surveys Sloan has commissioned to study online education in the United States, point to increasing enrollments and greater acceptance of online education. The Sloan survey concludes that enrollment in online courses continues to exceed that of the higher education population as a whole. According to the survey,

- over 4.6 million students took at least one online course during the fall 2008 term, which was a 17 percent increase over the number reported the previous year;
- the 17 percent growth rate for online enrollments far exceeds the 1.2 percent growth of the overall higher education student population; and
- more than one in four higher education students take at least one course online. (Allen and Seaman 2010, 1)

While the potential for online programs to grow exponentially is certainly possible, any new growth will more than likely occur among those institutions that already offer programs. According to an earlier Sloan survey: "Approximately one-third of higher education institutions account for three-quarters of all online enrollments. Future growth will come predominately from these and similar institutions as they add new programs and grow existing ones." Furthermore,

- although much of the past growth in online enrollments has been fueled by new institutions entering the online learning arena, this transition is now nearing its end; most institutions that plan to offer online education are already doing so;
- a large majority (69 percent) of academic leaders believe that student demand for online learning is still growing;
- a significant percentage (83 percent) of institutions with online offerings expect their online enrollments to increase over the coming year; and
- future growth in online enrollments will most likely come from those institutions that are currently the most engaged; they enroll the most online learning students and have the highest expectations for growth. (Allen and Seaman 2007, 2)

While these data are usefully suggestive of future trends in online education, understanding those trends means more than simply looking at enrollment rates and projecting those trend lines ever upward. What factors will determine whether and how online education continues to grow and thrive as a legitimate form of higher education? While it appears that growth rates are being sustained, what factors will determine whether online education remains an integral part of the higher education landscape or will be looked upon in hindsight as just an educational fad? There are five key drivers that will determine the future directions of online education: three-dimensional online education, the increasing acceptance of "disembodied" virtual interactions, the emergence of informal learning spaces, mass customization, and the globalization of online education.

Three-Dimensional Online Education

There is reason to believe that three-dimensional immersive spaces are the new face of the web and that in the very near future users will navigate web spaces rather than webpages. The most prominent recent example of such an immersive space is Second Life (SL), but three-dimensional online environments predate SL: multiuser virtual environments (MUVEs) have a history that dates to the mid-1990s. Indeed, SL might be thought of as an online version of *The Sims*, the popular life-simulation game produced by Electronic Arts. But SL has captured the attention of the business community and now the educational community, and it seems likely that the flat, two-dimensional webpage will be replaced by the three-dimensional web space.[1]

In SL, a user adopts an online persona in the form of an avatar. Users can craft their avatar into any form they wish: male or female, tall or short, even human or nonhuman. The users then navigate their avatar through the SL space, meeting up and conversing with other avatars (SL is not a war gaming site; in other such MUVEs, avatars are just as likely to start fighting each other). Residents can purchase (with real money) "real estate" within the SL space and then can build houses and office parks or any other kind of virtual structure they wish. Recently, large corporations such as Coca Cola, IBM, and Toyota have purchased real estate inside of SL; some businesses have tentatively begun to interview prospective candidates in a SL "virtual job fair." Like people who hide behind the mask of their avatars and play at different personas inside SL, businesses are similarly using the site as a way to play with different products and services, testing out and virtually marketing ideas that they might then launch in the real world (Hemp 2006).

Some organizations have purchased entire "islands" within SL where they can build multiple structures; indeed, institutions of higher education have taken a lead here in constructing virtual campuses. This is no small investment; these islands are purchased with real money, which might cost an institution tens of thousands of dollars, to say nothing of the technical staff needed to build and maintain structures on these islands. Some universities hope to use these virtual spaces to attract students, to allow them to "visit" the campus without the expense of an actual trip to the real campus (Joly 2007). It also seems likely that universities will use their virtual campuses as a way to stay connected with tech-savvy alumni.

Other universities are experimenting with SL as an educational space. Online education is sometimes criticized for removing the "face-to-face" element of the educational experience. It would seem that a virtual course in an SL-type environment would address some of these issues. A university might construct a virtual classroom or seminar room or theater within which a class of avatars might meet. Such a virtual classroom might replace the rather cumbersome chat function currently used in many distance education (DE) settings. Chats of more than a dozen or so people prove difficult to manage, as multiple threads of conversation become difficult to follow. In a virtual space, students in a three-dimensional setting might meet and mingle as in a real space, clustering together in groups to converse, work on group projects, or indeed just to listen to a lecture. As avatars become more expressive, body language and other nonverbal cues become possible, the lack of which in current online setups is often criticized as a major weakness of text-only interactions in online education. Virtual immersive spaces might provide DE students with a "feeling of presence" that they often lack in a learning environment that is built from just text and perhaps a still photograph (New Media Consortium and EDUCAUSE Learning Initiative 2007, 18).

MUVEs can also serve as a space for simulation and gaming. James Paul Gee and other scholars have drawn attention to the value of "serious games" for learning (Gee 2007). Spaces like SL allow for the creation of game and simulation environments where users can play with others simultaneously and at a distance. The National Oceanic and Atmospheric Administration (NOAA) has used its presence in SL to create a number of participatory simulations: users can fly into the eye of a hurricane, watch a glacier melt, or have a tsunami wash over them. Such phenomena cannot be directly experienced in real life without dire consequences, but in the virtual environment of SL the avatar "students" can actively experience them.

It is not too far a stretch to see other such applications, especially for history. Already, the Comparative Media Studies Lab at MIT has created "Revolution," a role-playing simulation of Colonial Williamsburg. A replica of the Roman Forum already exists in SL; Harlem in the 1920s has also been recreated.[2] "Life in a Medieval Town," "The Lowell Mills," and "The Energy Crisis" are all possible historical simulations that might be created in an SL-type environment. Because of the nature of the MUVE, the benefits of these active, participatory, three-dimensional learning objects need not be confined to a particular location, the very definition of an online education experience. As a pedagogical space, MUVEs allow avatars to participate and to experience.

The excitement generated by SL has been tempered by the realization that, while SL claims millions of residents, very few avatars seem to be present inside SL at any given time. Some residents observe that the sites and islands of SL seem almost deserted, technical glitches and a steep learning curve being possible reasons for this lack of participation. While SL as a specific destination might indeed be a fad, it is very likely that immersive, interactive, participatory three-dimensional spaces will in fact become the norm on the Internet; in the not too distant future, all users of the web will have their own avatar that will navigate within three-dimensional spaces. A three-dimensional Blackboard, WebCT, or other course management system seems just on the horizon.

Increasing Acceptance of "Disembodied" Virtual Interactions

Philosopher Hubert L. Dreyfus observes: "Only in a classroom where the teacher and learner sense that they are taking risks in each other's presence, and each can count on criticism from the other, are the conditions present that promote acquiring proficiency, and only by acting in the real world can one acquire expertise." This argument would seem to rule out DE as an effective means of education. "As for the apprenticeship necessary to become a master," Dreyfus concludes, "it is only possible where the learner sees the day-to-day responses of a master and learns to imitate her style" (2001, 92). According to Dreyfus, then, the best teaching occurs only via "embodied" interaction between teachers and students.

Yet there is a wide variety of "disembodied" interactions that we find legitimate and effective forms of education. For instance, you are reading a book right now and, I hope, learning asynchronously, to use the language of DE, without needing to be sitting next to the author. Listening to a recording of a concert is a disembodied interaction, and yet a perfectly valid and useful way to experience music. Very few scholars would argue that they should give up writing books and articles as a way to advance scholarship and devote themselves strictly to conference presentations because the latter are more "embodied" than the "disembodied" interactions of books and articles.

That claim for embodied interaction as superior to disembodied interaction certainly does not seem to hold true for today's millennial generation, who seem more comfortable with virtual relationships than baby boomers or even their Generation-Y parents. We have all had the experience of passing someone on the street holding a very private cell phone conversation in a very public place. People over the age of forty often complain that people are being impolite or disrespectful when they interrupt a face-to-face conversation in order to answer a cell phone or respond to the "ping" of some electronic device. Although increasingly true for people of all ages, at times, it seems, young people especially are more engaged with their electronic devices than with the physical world surrounding them. The popular comic strip *Zits* often captures this generational divide: in a recent cartoon, two teenagers sit a foot or so apart while maddeningly tapping away at small handheld devices. In the midst of their furious tapping, the two stop, exchange a short kiss, remark, "The time we spend together is so precious," and then return to their electronic devices. (I have actually witnessed my son and his girlfriend engaged in such behavior.) Older generations are mystified by the idea that the "friends" on a MySpace page are in any way like real friends; only when people can go to a restaurant or attend a dinner party together can they claim legitimate, real friendship. To many of us over the age of forty, electronic friendships do not appear like real friendships at all, but such disembodied experiences are as real and important to the current young generation as the face-to-face embodied interactions that their elders prefer.

Young people today inhabit two worlds: a physical world and a virtual networked world. When they step out of a conversation to accept a cell phone call or when they text-message their friends or play a multiplayer online game, these students, in effect, are entering into a virtual world while they remain physically present (if detached) in the real world. I am in no way excusing or condoning impolite behavior; I am only trying to understand the worldview of young people today and to anticipate the meaning and implications of such behavior for the future. Nor am I suggesting that disembodied interactions will in any way displace embodied interactions in the lives of our students. I am claiming, however, that these virtual, disembodied interactions and experiences are as real to these students and as valued as their embodied, face-to-face relationships.

This trend has clear implications for the future of online education. As more millennials enter higher education, and as more millennials mature into nontraditional students, they will approach online education with fewer concerns than perhaps an earlier generation of students might. More important, as millennials themselves become professors, teaching in an online, disembodied fashion will not seem at all disorienting to them. Faculty buy-in has long been one of the key drivers in the acceptance and success of online education programs; there is reason to suspect that for the next generation of professors, online teaching will not pose a significant problem, since their disembodied interactions with students will seem to them just as natural and fulfilling and meaningful as their face-to-face interactions.

Informal Learning Spaces

Faculty at some colleges and universities are making the class materials for their courses—lecture notes, PowerPoint slides, syllabi, reading lists—available freely on the Internet. MIT's OpenCourseWare project is perhaps the most notable example of this open-source ethic, but an increasing number of professors' lectures are being uploaded to YouTube and receiving several thousand hits, suggesting that there is a demand among students for online, freely available learning materials. Those who are accessing these materials from the MIT site are not receiving course credit or other kinds of credentials, which suggests that a new kind of online, informal learning might be emerging that will exist alongside more formal, credentialed learning.

Emblematic of this informal learning, the Wikiversity may well represent to higher education what Wikipedia has meant to the traditional encyclopedia. Created in 2006 by the same people who created Wikipedia, the Wikiversity (http://wikiversity.org) is similar to MIT's OpenCourse-Ware project in that it is a collection of learning materials made freely available to anyone on the Internet. Unlike MIT's project, these learning materials are produced by the participants of the Wikiversity, who, like their counterparts in the Wikipedia, are committed volunteers. Another important difference is that the courses at the Wikiversity are organized and led by course leaders who achieve their positions by virtue of their reputations and their prior contributions to Wikiversity courses, not necessarily because of any degree credentials. An online course via Wikiversity, then, looks very much like an online course offered by a traditional university except that it is "open" in every sense of the word, from admissions criteria and the creation of the "textbooks" and other learning objects to the choice of the leader who is privileged to teach the course.

It is unlikely that the Wikiversity, or any imitators that might emerge, will replace the traditional university any time soon. Nor will Wikiversity entirely replace the model of online learning that has developed over the last decade. However, informal learning spaces will undoubtedly provide an alternative learning environment for many people, especially those seeking lifelong learning options. Retiring baby boomers may want to spend part of their retirement savings and intellectual vigor on education as leisure. An informal online learning environment—without the pressure or need for traditional credentialing—will be attractive to these students. Free access to education might also prove attractive to those who understand the need for higher education, but who lack the financial resources to take advantage of it.

Like Wikipedia, Wikiversity is dependent upon the contributions of volunteers. If Wikiversity does thrive, it will be because a new type of professoriate will have emerged: those who teach for their personal benefit or for some other benefit, but not necessarily because a university is paying them. This amateur professoriate might look something like the model that has developed at the University of Phoenix, where most of the teaching faculty are low-paid adjuncts. Their low pay is justified since these adjuncts are professionals in their fields who do not necessarily need to teach for remuneration. Instead, they view teaching as a form of pro bono volunteer work.

This model of an informal, online learning space with course leaders who teach pro bono would have implications for professors in the humanities, who typically do not have professional careers outside of the academy and who in fact define their professions in terms of the academy. However, it is also possible that informal, online learning spaces would serve as an extension or outreach activity for traditional universities: the "free college" that is provided to the public in an online environment and taught by university faculty. There would be no grades or credits offered by this free college, whose students would be motivated only by their desire to learn.

Mass Customization

There is much talk about how our current educational system is based too much on a nineteenth-century industrial model and how education today must align to the new digital, networked, twenty-first-century realities. Many of these same reformers also speak of the need for increased standardization in learning objectives, curriculum and, importantly, assessment. However, the idea of standardization is quintessentially nineteenth-century and industrial in its orientation. If education is indeed to align to twenty-first-century realties, it would seem that mass customization would be the real reform.

"Mass customization," a term that comes from manufacturing, means that customers can tailor products to meet their individual needs. In preindustrial life, this is how much manufacturing occurred: customers would go to the local blacksmith or tailor and request a product made to their specifications. (These are described as "bespoken goods" by economic historians.) This system of localized production meant, of course, that relatively small numbers of goods could be made. With the advent of industrialization, factories could produce a much larger number of goods, but at the cost of the loss of individually tailored products. The products of the assembly line were one-size-fits-all, the same iteration again and again, each product "standardized" for easier, more efficient mass production. In contrast, economists today speak of mass customization, whereby the same techniques that can quickly and efficiently produce a lot of goods can also be tailored to meet individual customer demands. Mass customization has become especially prevalent in the service sector. Consider the kinds of individually tailored services that Amazon provides to all of its customers: I receive monthly selections based on my personal buying habits, selections tailored to my previous individual choices.

The history of education parallels these developments in manufacturing. Before mass schooling, an individual student would study with an individual master or tutor. That teacher might work with only a handful of students; indeed, the British tutorial system is in many ways a legacy of this preindustrial approach to education. This was the era of customized education. Mass schooling mirrored the rise of the factory (hence the factory model school); schools would educate larger and larger numbers of students, each of whom would receive the same, standardized education. But this also meant that students would be treated as the same, measured against the same standards.

What if the technologies of online education allowed for mass customization in higher education? Currently, individualized education is usually reserved for special-needs children; districts must create special curricula to ensure that the educational needs of these students are met. Often, these educational goals have distinct features that do not match up with the goals for other students. The increasing number of homeschooled students (whose parents make this choice not solely for religious reasons) also get an individualized education, and it is not a coincidence that the homeschool movement has been interested in online learning.

What if all education, even higher education, was conceived in this fashion?[3] What if all students, of all types of ability, were able to customize their own learning objectives and assessments? In theory, no two students would have the same educational experience or even the same educational objectives and outcomes. As imagined by the Knowledge-Works Foundation and the Institute for the Future, customized education would mean that "personalized learning plans will leverage new media, brain research, and school structures to create differentiated learning experiences based on individual needs" (KnowledgeWorks 2010). This image of the future refers specifically to K–12 education, but it is easy to see the implications for higher education: online education might become a vehicle for delivering personalized, customizable education to a large number of students. In such a mass customization system, more responsibility for learning would fall on the student, and students in such a system would need to be highly self-directed and exhibit great initiative, all of which well describes the characteristics of many of today's students who take classes online.

There are, of course, significant barriers at the moment that could keep this vision of the future from occurring. Many professional organizations, for example, are developing mandatory curricula for certification. So too are the accreditation associations for business programs and the sciences. In such a setting, there is little to no room for individualized curricula. Moreover, universities find it more cost-effective to offer multiple, identical sections of fewer courses. Only when these institutional factors change will the vision of a mass customized education emerge.

Globalization of Online Education

Like so many other economic sectors, higher education is feeling the impact of the forces of globalization. This takes a variety of forms, each reflecting the differing meanings of the term *globalization*. The demand for higher education is a global phenomenon, and as a result the demand for higher education "services" is no longer contained behind national boundaries. More and more American universities, for example, are setting up collaborative agreements with universities in other parts of the world; in effect, American institutions are establishing "regional" campuses across the globe, especially in the Middle East, India, and China. Online education is a typical first step in the process of establishing a presence in the global higher education market; consider the model represented by the University of Maryland University College, with an online presence in Europe and Asia (although, admittedly, aimed at Americans stationed there). The University of Phoenix, having already expanded across the United States, seeks to offer online classes across the world. At present, the American brand of higher education is still the world leader, and countries like China—as it does for other commercial goods—represent an enormous potential market of students. American online colleges could very well meet this global demand.

But with the rise to economic prominence of China, India, Brazil, and other nations, we might well also see a challenge to America's preeminent role as a higher education leader. Chinese universities, for example, have been expanding their own online education programs, or Internet colleges. The number and scope of these colleges is not at present near the levels found in the United States, but their growing numbers and, importantly, their growing acceptance in China means that they could represent a major global competitor to U.S.-based online education. A Chinese version of the University of Phoenix, for example, might start to attract not only students from China but also students from the United States, especially for the language classes not offered by U.S. universities.

In addition to expanding the potential market for students, it is also possible that online education from the non-Western world could represent an important new market for teachers; globalization reflects not only a global competition for students, but also a potential global supply of teachers. In an online world, where teaching and learning are asynchronous and not location-specific, it does not really matter if the teacher or the students are located in Illinois or in India. To readers in the Western world: it is entirely possible that your next online teaching job will be working for a Chinese-based online college (Zhao, Zhang, and Li 2006).

We know that adjuncts and other contingent faculty teach the majority of online classes and that many of them feel marginalized as little more than high-tech indentured servants. As the global supply of online faculty grows and as these adjuncts become more organized, might we see increasing labor volatility in this supply? Like other areas of online education, the organization and unionization of online teachers have also been globalized. The Coalition of Contingent Academic Labor (COCAL) has been organizing adjuncts from the United States, Canada, and Mexico, "and the movement has been successful in building solidarity and resulting in increased visibility and gains for wages through local unionizing campaigns," writes Eileen Schell (2007). Many of these online adjuncts are organized via "open-source unionism," which Julie M. Schmid (2004) describes as

> a form of unionization that uses Web technology to organize in hard-to-unionize workplaces. Rather than depend on the traditional means of union organizing—leafleting at the plant gate, holding organizing meetings in the break room, or "house visiting" workers after hours, for example—open-source union organizing relies on "cybertools" such as Listservs, chat rooms, and Web sites. These tools help bring together people who, as a result of the new economy, are employed at separate locations, often as temporary or contract workers, and lack a common work experience.

Like the open-source software movement—in which communities of programmers linked through the Internet share and improve upon software code—open-source unionism embraces the utopian, collaborative ethos of the Internet revolution. Ideas and calls-to-action are circulated over the Web, shared ideologies are developed through e-mail exchanges, and, through this process, a nascent worker consciousness is forged.

A global union of online educators would be a natural outcome of the globalization of higher education.

Of course, before any of this happens, a host of issues related to accreditation, quality assurance, and degree granting across national boundaries would need to be settled. What if a global agency—perhaps tied to UNESCO—began to monitor and regulate the globalization of online education, much as the World Bank, the World Trade Organization, and other such international arrangements have been harmonizing economic activities in other sectors? Might something like a transnational agency emerge that will be tasked with smoothing accreditation procedures across national borders? What of the regulation of such international transactions? Might a similar sort of agency or consortium of universities seek to establish regulations? We are already seeing some signs of this kind of transnational regulation of higher education: the Bologna Accords, signed in 1999 and implemented in March 2010, established a uniform set of degree standards among universities in the member states of the European Union (www.eha.info). Similar international agreements in online education programs would make credit transfer between different online colleges easier. Such an international accord would ensure an ever-growing number of online programs.

International harmonization of online education might also be based on the model emerging from the Whitney International University System. Bermuda-based Whitney has either acquired controlling stakes in or established alliances between private universities (most recently establishing a presence in Latin America). This model establishes transfer agreements between the institutions owned by Whitney, agreements across national borders (Campbell 2008). The model of international regulation and transfer agreements might just as easily come from for-profit corporations as from international agencies and nongovernmental organizations.

Not only would there need to be an international system to regulate credit transfers and quality assurance, but cultural issues would also need to be considered. As online classes become more internationalized, what idioms will emerge to unite students of different countries and cultures taking the same online courses together? Will there emerge an online educational creole that will facilitate this conversation between different cultures?[4] Perhaps a virtual reality online setting (described above) will lead to the creation of such a digital creole? These issues of accreditation, harmonization of standards, and negotiation of cultural differences will need to be addressed, for if growth in online learning is to be sustainable, it will be because the market for online education has expanded beyond the borders of the United States.

Conclusion

The future of online education must be understood as more than simply an upward trend line of increasing enrollments. The five trends identified here suggest that the very nature and practice of online education will be altered over the next few years: in how teaching and learning will occur, in how online education will be managed and organized, and, most importantly, in how the meaning of "education" in online environments will be understood.

Notes

1. For an interesting introduction to online environments, see Castronova (2005).

2. For Revolution, see www.educationarcade.org/node/357; for the Roman Forum, see http://secondlife.com/destination/roman-forum; for Virtual Harlem, see http://slurl.com/secondlife/Virtual%20Harlem/41/35/30/?title=Welcome%20to%20Virtual%20Harlem&msg=Virtual%20Harlem%2C%20focusing%20on%20the%20Jazz%20Age/Harlem%20Renaissance%20of%20the%201920s.

3. Governor Michael O. Leavitt of Utah already envisioned such an idea in 1999 (Carr 1999).

4. See the World Bank's East Asia Global Distance Education Network Site for what this might look like. www.ouhk.edu.hk/cridal/gdenet/.

References

Allen, I. Elaine, and Jeff Seaman. 2007. *Online Nation: Five Years of Growth in Online Learning.* Sloan Consortium. October. www.sloan-c.org/publications/survey/online_nation.

———. 2010. *Learning on Demand: Online Education in the United States, 2009.* Sloan Consortium. January. www.sloan-c.org/publications/survey/learning_on_demand_sr2010.

Campbell, Monica. 2008. "A Texas Company Sees Online Learning as Growth Industry in Latin America." *Chronicle of Higher Education,* September 12. http://chronicle.com/weekly/v55/i03/03a02701.htm.

Carr, Sarah. "Look to Customization, Utah Governor Says." *Chronicle of Higher Education*, November 5, 1999. http://chronicle.com/weekly/v46/i11/11a05702. htm.

Castronova, Edward. 2005. *Synthetic World: The Business and Culture of Online Games*. Chicago: University of Chicago Press.

Dreyfus, Hubert L. 2001. *On the Internet*. London: Routledge.

Gee, James Paul. 2003. *What Video Games Have to Teach Us About Learning and Literacy*. New York: Palgrave Macmillan.

Hemp, Paul. 2006. "Avatar-Based Marketing," *Harvard Business Review* 84, no. 6: 48–57.

Joly, Karine. 2007. "A Second Life for Higher Education?" *University Business* (June): 62.

KnowledgeWorks Foundation and the Institute for the Future. 2010. "Map of Future Forces Affecting Education." www.kwfdn.org/map/map.aspx.

New Media Consortium and EDUCAUSE Learning Initiative. 2007. *The Horizon Report*. www.nmc.org/pdf/2007_Horizon_Report.pdf.

Schell, Eileen. 2007. "Online Education, Contingent Faculty, and Open-Source Unionism." March 18. www.edu-factory.org/index.php?option=com_content& task=view&id=44&Itemid=33.

Schmid, Julie M. 2004. "Open-Source Unionism: New Workers, New Strategies." *Academe Online* (January–February). www.aaup.org/AAUP/pubsres/ academe/2004/JF/Feat/schm.htm.

Zhao, Yong, Gaoming Zhang, and Ning Li. 2006. "The Life of 'Internet Colleges': Policies, Problems, and Prospects of Online Higher Education in China." *EDUCAUSE Review* 41, no. 6: 48–59. http://connect.educause.edu/Library/ EDUCAUSE+Review/TheLifeofInternetColleges/40672.

About the Contributors

Melanie L. Buffington is currently an assistant professor of art education at Virginia Commonwealth University. Her research interests primarily relate to Web 2.0 technology in education, museum education, multiculturalism, teaching research methodologies, and teacher preparation. Before earning her MA and PhD at Ohio State University, she was a middle school art teacher. Currently, she is collaborating with a coworker on a book for practicing teachers about research in art education settings.

Sharmila Pixy Ferris is a professor in the Department of Communication at William Paterson University of New Jersey, where she also serves as director of the Center for Teaching Excellence. Her research brings an interdisciplinary focus to computer-mediated communication and educational technologies. She has published several books in these areas, as well as in a number of journals, both print and online.

Daryl E. Fridley is an assistant professor in the Department of History at Southeast Missouri State University, where he coordinates the social studies teacher preparation program and teaches courses in social studies education and history. When he was teaching in public schools, a lack of access to traditional primary source materials spurred his initial online search for resources. Over the ensuing years it became clear that using Internet resources held additional benefits, and he regularly encourages teacher candidates in social studies to take full advantage of them. His primary research focus is the improvement of social studies teacher preparation in the context of a democratic society.

Allen C. Gathman is a professor of biology and director of the Center for Writing Excellence at Southeast Missouri State University. He teaches a variety of courses in biology, particularly in genetics, as well as an honors science and religion class. He developed and first taught the online version of the Biology Department's introductory course in 1999 and has been teaching online regularly since then. During that time, he has incorporated more online elements into his face-to-face classes. For his biological research in bioinformatics he uses online databases, plus maintains some of his own for use by others. Recognizing the growing importance of online information in his field, in the spring of 2010 he began teaching his molecular genetics class with no print textbook, substituting online resources. His students are incrementally developing a class genetics wiki as a teaching and learning tool, and both online and face-to-face students use Facebook to ask him questions.

Martha Henckell is an adjunct professor for the Harrison College of Business and College of Education, as well as the information technology director of User Services at Southeast Missouri State University. In these positions she has the opportunity to work in two interlaced and exciting fields: education and technology. Publishing credits include *Evaluation of Distance Education: The Student Perspective* (2008) and coauthorship of several encyclopedia articles. Her latest online initiative is building short and simple administrative system web courses for Southeast faculty and staff.

Steven J. Hoffman is a professor of history and coordinator of the historic preservation program at Southeast Missouri State University, where he teaches classes in public history, historic preservation, and African-American history. His publications include *Race, Class and Power in the Building of Richmond, 1870–1920* (2004) and articles on southern urban history and the use of technology in the teaching of history. He is an associate editor of the *Journal of the Association of History and Computing*.

Michelle Kilburn is an assistant professor in the Department of Criminal Justice and Sociology at Southeast Missouri State University. She has published articles pertaining to online learning in the *Encyclopedia of Online and Distance Education, Encyclopedia of Information and Technology*, and *Human Systems Management*. Before becoming an assistant professor, she was the first director of online programs at the university. Her areas of interest are students' perceptions of online learning and pedagogical foundations of online learning.

Lisa M. Lane has been a history instructor at MiraCosta College in California since 1989 and has been teaching online for over a decade. As founder of MiraCosta's Program for Online Teaching, she works with both novice and experienced online instructors and emphasizes the pedagogical foundations of distance education. She writes and blogs on issues of interest to online professors, instructional technologists, and teachers. She holds a master's in history from the University of California, Santa Barbara, and an online teaching certificate from UCLA.

Khadijah O. Miller is an assistant professor and chair of the Department of Interdisciplinary Studies in the College of Liberal Arts at Norfolk State University, which offers the only fully online Bachelor of Science degree at NSU. Her doctorate in African-American studies serves as an impetus for her love of interdisciplinarity and impacts her research interests, which include online learning, interdisciplinarity, and African-American studies; and the survival and thriving tactics of African-American women. She has published in the *Journal of American History,* the *Journal of African American History*, and with the encyclopedia series of Salem Press. She is currently working on a project that focuses on the work/life balance dynamics of African-American women.

Maureen C. Minielli is an assistant professor at Kingsborough Community College, CUNY, in Brooklyn, New York. Her research interests include rhetorical theory and criticism, the history of communication studies as an academic discipline, and computer mediated communication. She is the author of several articles and book chapters primarily focused on the use of technology in higher education.

Peter Sands is an associate professor in the University of Wisconsin-Milwaukee Department of English, teaching graduate and undergraduate courses in American literature, rhetoric, science fiction, and utopianism. A longtime advocate for networked computing in teaching and scholarship, he coedited *Electronic Collaboration in the Humanities* (2003); has published in *Academic.Writing*, *ACE Journal*, *Kairos*, *Utopian Studies*, *Works and Days*, and elsewhere; and is founding editor of H-Utopia, part of the Humanities and Social Sciences Online network (http://h-net. org). Having recently completed a JD, he is currently writing about law, rhetoric, and utopia, while maintaining an active interest in new media legal issues.

David J. Staley is an adjunct associate professor and director of the Harvey Goldberg Center for Excellence in Teaching in the Department of History at Ohio State University. From 2003 to 2008, he served as the executive director of the American Association for History and Computing. He is the author of *Computers, Visualization and History* (2003) and *History and Future: Using Historical Thinking to Imagine the Future* (2007). He is principal of the DStaley Group, a strategic foresight consulting firm.

Mary Harriet Talbut has been an instructor in the Department of Middle and Secondary Education at Southeast Missouri State University since 1997 and has been teaching as well as taking courses online for over a decade. She also works with teacher candidates on incorporating technology into their classroom best practices. She taught social studies in a small rural school when technology was being introduced to the district. She is a doctoral candidate in curriculum and instruction in social studies from the University of Missouri, Columbia. In addition to technology and its uses in the classroom, her research interests include the Teacher Work Sample Methodology and rural education.

Index